LAURA McCABE'S
EMBELLISHED BEADWEAVING

LAURA McCABE'S
EMBELLISHED BEADWEAVING

JEWELRY LAVISHED WITH FRINGE, FRONDS, LACEWORK & MORE

LARK BOOKS

A Division of Sterling Publishing Co., Inc.

New York / London

For my Mick

Editor
Nathalie Mornu

Art Director
Kristi Pfeffer

Illustrator
J'aime Allene

Photographer
Stewart O'Shields

Cover Designer
Celia Naranjo

Technical Editors
Greg Hanson and Marcie Stone

Editorial Assistant
Kathleen McCafferty

Art Production Assistant
Bradley Norris

Library of Congress Cataloging-in-Publication Data

McCabe, Laura.
  Laura McCabe's embellished beadweaving : jewelry lavished with fringe, fronds, lacework & more / Laura McCabe. -- 1st ed.
    p. cm.
  Includes index.
  ISBN 978-1-60059-514-1 (hc-plc with jacket : alk. paper)
  1. Beadwork. 2. Weaving. 3. Jewelry making. I. Title. II. Title: Embellished beadweaving.
  TT860.M372 2010
  745.594'2--dc22

                                    2009037579

10 9 8 7 6 5 4 3 2 1

First Edition

Published by Lark Books, A Division of
Sterling Publishing Co., Inc.
387 Park Avenue South, New York, NY 10016

Text © 2010, Laura Jean McCabe
Photography © 2010, Lark Books, a Division of Sterling Publishing Co., Inc.,
unless otherwise specified
Illustrations © 2010, Lark Books, a Division of Sterling Publishing Co., Inc.

Distributed in Canada by Sterling Publishing,
c/o Canadian Manda Group, 165 Dufferin Street
Toronto, Ontario, Canada M6K 3H6

Distributed in the United Kingdom by GMC Distribution Services,
Castle Place, 166 High Street, Lewes, East Sussex, England BN7 1XU

Distributed in Australia by Capricorn Link (Australia) Pty Ltd.,
P.O. Box 704, Windsor, NSW 2756 Australia

If you have questions or comments about this book, please contact:
Lark Books
67 Broadway
Asheville, NC 28801
828-253-0467

Manufactured in China

ISBN 13: 978-1-60059-514-1

For information about custom editions, special sales, or premium and corporate purchases, please contact the Sterling Special Sales Department at 800-805-5489 or specialsales@sterlingpub.com.

For information about desk and examination copies available to college and university professors, requests must be submitted to academic@larkbooks.com. Our complete policy can be found at www.larkbooks.com.

CONTENTS

INTRODUCTION

EMBELLISH MEANS TO DECORATE, TO ENHANCE, TO ADD BEAUTY THROUGH ORNAMENTATION OR FANCIFUL DETAILS. AND BEADWORK IS, FUNDAMENTALLY, THE EMBODIMENT OF EMBELLISHMENT. BEADS HAVE EXISTED IN ONE FORM OR ANOTHER IN VIRTUALLY EVERY CULTURE. BEADS AND BEADWORK ARE ONE OF THE EARLIEST FORMS OF PERSONAL ADORNMENT THAT DECORATE BOTH THE BODY AND ITS BELONGINGS. FROM THE EARLIEST DAYS OF MAN THROUGH TO MODERN TIMES, HUMANS HAVE USED BEADS TO ENHANCE THE BEAUTY OF THE OBJECTS THEY POSSESS AND TO HEIGHTEN THEIR OWN ATTRACTIVENESS.

If we accept that beads are the manifestation of embellishment, the next logical question is, why? Why do we choose to enhance our world and ourselves with these simple yet intriguing objects? Beads are unique because they reach beyond the realm of simple decoration. They hold more valuable meanings. People have used beads (and continue to use them) to convey wealth and social status, to make tangible the religious concepts of prayer, and even to protect their wearer from evil spirits and to bring good fortune.

Having established what beads are and why we use them, one question remains: how? How do we use these beads to their best advantage, to make ourselves beautiful and add fanciful details to our world?

That's the aim of this book: to provide the knowledge and inspiration to take your beadwork to the next level by embellishing beads with yet more beads—to create a multidimensional realm of beauty and adornment, all made possible by starting with one single bead. Chapters 1, 2, and 3 give you the foundations you'll need to get started, but chapter 4 gets to the heart of the matter, providing a vast array of embellishment forms that are then applied to the 18 projects that follow. These projects have been created with the intent to inspire, foster, and encourage creativity on a personal level, but they're also meant to educate you on the application of embellishment forms in larger beaded jewelry and to provide both visual and technical inspiration. And in case you want to see still more, check out the gallery images—of both my work and that of artists working with similar techniques—sprinkled throughout the book.

Over the past 17 years, my personal and professional explorations into the world of beads have given me a great appreciation for the history, creativity, and devotion contained in beadweaving. This book shares the techniques inspired by the lavish beauty of the natural world. Every embellishment form taught here was inspired by plants or animals, both common and exotic, in all of their remarkable and sometimes unconventional beauty.

Although I give you step-by-step instructions, don't feel you have to reproduce the projects in this book exactly; instead, use them as basic building blocks for your own embellished forms. I genuinely hope you'll take what you learn here and apply it liberally to your own creative endeavors.

CHAPTER ONE

BEADS
THROUGH
HISTORY

The age-old human fascination with beads remains something of an enigma. in addition to their aesthetic beauty, beads have served as a symbol of spiritual protection, religious conviction, and social status. They always have—and always will—embellish our bodies, our lives, and our souls in a way that no other object can. Beads as valued human possessions have existed since the dawn of man and can be found in virtually every culture throughout history and across the world, some dating as far back as 40,000 years.

Initially, early man collected objects with natural holes, such as stones and seashells, and strung these objects on sinew in order to wear them. Their significance remains pure speculation, but it's likely they were worn as protective amulets and as a means of connecting with the natural world. Early beads were frequently made using bone, shell, and stone. Hammer stones formed the basic shape; beads were drilled using stone points, and refined using beach sand with water or horsetail grasses. The labor-intensive nature of these objects gave them an intrinsic value that led to their use as currency in many cultures around the globe.

In Africa, more than any other place on earth, beads as an indication of social status were (and continue to be) a fundamental element in body adornment. From the highly developed civilizations of ancient Egypt to the small hunter-gatherer tribes that inhabited the farthest reaches of the continent, beads were paramount in conveying wealth and social status. The materials used to make them often reflected the resources of the particular group making the beads. Seed and stone beads are common among the more primitive tribesmen,

while more technologically complex beads, such as fabricated metal beads and faience, are found among the advanced civilizations of Africa.

As bead- and jewelry-making skills were refined and technologies developed, beads became diverse in color, shape, and type, but their fundamental significance remained the same. Throughout the ancient world, in Phoenicia, Egypt, Greece, and Rome, in the Americas and in the Far East, beads served as spiritually significant religious objects and were appreciated for their monetary value.

Beads continued to hold these values throughout the Middle Ages, particularly for members of the Catholic Church, in the form of rosary beads, and Muslims, who carried prayer beads. As clothing became more ornate during the Renaissance, the use of beads as embellishment on fabric became much more prominent. Among royalty and the upper echelons of society, beaded embellishment went so far as to include precious stones such as diamonds, rubies, emer-

Laura McCabe
Third Eye, 2002
Length, 48.3 cm

Glass doll's eyes, glass seed beads, freshwater pearls, antique Italian micro beads, antique metal button, leather; embroidery, peyote stitch, lacy stitch, embellishment

PHOTO BY MELINDA HOLDEN

alds, sapphires, and pearl beads on clothing. The wardrobe of Queen Elizabeth I is an excellent example of this ostentatious form of embellishment.

In the New World, the tradition of beads continued. As the contact between Native Americans, European explorers, and religious refugees increased, bone, shell, and stone beads were replaced with glass "trade beads" (as they became known) from Europe. At that time in history, beads became very valuable as a means of trade. Early hunters traded beads for furs; later, trade beads substituted for currency. In fact, until 1637, beads remained a form of legal tender in the state of Connecticut.

As the traditions of Europe were brought to the New World via the colonists, so were beads and bead artistry. Although the Puritans of New England maintained a lifestyle of extreme modesty in their personal dress, they made ornate beaded objects for use in the home. Native Americans applied their skills, learned from traditional quill work techniques, to the tiny glass beads from Europe. The result was amazingly intricate embroidery on purses, ceremonial objects, and clothing.

During the Victorian era, the use of beads on clothing came into favor in both Europe and the United States. Native Americans continued to bead using small glass beads, and the various objects they made—including purses, belts, pincushions, and pillows—became popular souvenirs for those traveling westward.

There are numerous examples of intricately beaded clothing, textiles, and accessories from the late Victorian era that pay tribute to the fine craft of bead embroidery, bead crochet, and beadweaving. Beaded

Two examples of late 19th century crochet purses made from tiny microbeads. In both cases, the beads were strung up first and then woven into elaborate patterns, row by row. Purses like these are a remarkable example of perfection and attention to detail in beadwork. Note the tiny sapphires in the closure on the purse frame at right.

purses became very popular during this era, and there are many examples of these accessories made with both glass beads and steel-cut beads. The steel cuts are machine-made beads originating in France, and they were made until about 1930. Bombing that occurred during the war destroyed the factories where these beautiful beads were made, and to this day they remain out of production.

The use of beads remained prominent in fashion throughout the 1920s. Heavily beaded dresses marked the elaborate and risqué styles of the flapper era. These trends continued into the '30s and '40s, although the Great Depression had an impact on the world of fashion.

While beads continue to be popular today, the trend of lavish adornment characterized by earlier eras remains unmatched. In a world that values immediate gratification and disposability over the cost and labor of fine craftsmanship, many of these ancient techniques are beginning to fade. It's my hope that by recording these historic beading techniques and traditions we can appreciate the past and discover inspiration for the future.

Laura McCabe

Peach & Cream Laguna Bracelet, 2008

19 x 5.1 cm

Laguna agate by Gary Wilson, glass seed beads, Japanese keshi pearls, freshwater pearls, crystal beads, leather; embroidery, peyote stitch, embellishment

PHOTO BY MELINDA HOLDEN

Left, examples of Victorian-era appliqués that were beaded on tulle and then stitched onto clothing afterward. These were made with glass beads intended to look like real jet. Below, Victorian-era wrist warmers crocheted with white glass seed beads added during the process.

CHAPTER TWO

BASIC BEADING KIT

When it comes to the beader's toolbox, the options for equipment are endless, and more and more tools are constantly entering the marketplace.

Tools

Several basic tools are must-haves for all beaders and are required, to some degree or another, for the projects in this book.

Beading Needles

The rule of thumb for beading needles is that the larger the number, the thinner the needle. The most common sizes for beading needles are 10, 12, 13, and, occasionally, 15. My own preference is for English beading needles; they hold up better to my stitching and are a little bit thinner than other commercial brands.

Scissors

Three basic styles are useful. Choose a sharp pair of embroidery scissors for snipping threads as close to the beadwork as possible. Sewing shears are helpful for beadweaving projects that require larger cuts. Use them to cut leather, Ultrasuede, or material. Finally, because some of the beading threads, notably FireLine, cause rapid dulling of scissors, keep a pair of cheap scissors on hand for cutting these threads.

No-Tangle Bobbins

No-tangle bobbins are great little tools for keeping your work orderly, especially if you travel with it. They pop open so tail threads can be wrapped around the spool, then snap shut, keeping your thread neatly wound. While you're working on a piece, they help separate and keep aside threads you're not immediately beading with.

Thread Burner

Originally used as medical cauterizers, battery-powered thread burners can help eliminate tiny tails or thread fuzz left on the finished work. Take care when handling one of these—the filament gets very hot and can burn you.

Chain-Nose Pliers

Chain-nose pliers work well to break extra beads out, and come in handy when you have trouble pulling a needle through a stubborn bead.

Measuring Tape

A measuring tape is very useful when determining the size of a finished piece or the spacing of beads within a piece. The classic dressmaker's tape works best and fits easily into your tool kit.

Beading Board

A good work surface makes all the difference when beading. A velvet bead board works well to prevent beads from rolling away. Among the variety of commercial beading surfaces, the most common is the Vellux fabric square. These are portable and take up very little space when packed; the downside is that you need to pick up everything before you move on to another location. There are also bead boards available that close up, to contain the beads while you're mid-project.

Task Lamp

Good lighting is essential, and standard tungsten and fluorescent lights won't allow you to properly perceive true color. Look for task lamps that provide low wattage with natural, full-spectrum light.

Materials

Although bead requirements vary from project to project, you'll want to always keep the following basic materials in your toolbox.

Beading Threads

FireLine is a brand of fishing line that works well for beading and holds up to sharp-edged beads such as crystals. It comes in a variety of weights and colors; I tend to use 6-lb. weight (sometimes also denoted as size D or .006"/0.15 mm), and I stick to crystal and smoke. The smoke color has a black oil coating, which makes it messy to work with, but a pre-wax washing helps remove some of the oil from the line. Just run the threaded strand through a paper towel with a little warm water and dish soap, and run it through a clean dry towel a few times before waxing. To make threading the needle a little easier, flatten the ends with your fingernails or a pair of pliers. **Tip:** With the crystal FireLine, color the tip of your thread with a permanent marker so it's easy to see when threading.

There's an extensive array of nylon beading threads. Although there's some variation from brand to brand, most are good, durable threads for many types of beading projects. Nylon threads don't hold up to sharp beads the way FireLine does, but they're perfectly suitable for projects using glass seed beads, pressed glass beads, or pearls. They have a soft hand and work well in creating fluid and organic embellishments on beadwork.

Microcrystalline Wax

Of the various types of thread-conditioning agents available, I like to use microcrystalline wax, a synthetic, man-made wax. It coats your thread to prevent tangles and makes knots easier to undo. It also coats you hands, which helps protect the beads from your body oils and creates a better tension due to the "stickiness factor." Because the wax melts at a much lower temperature than beeswax does, you can wipe off excess wax from your beadwork using a paper towel dipped in hot water. Unlike beeswax, which is organic, microcrystalline wax remains stable over time and won't cause thread rot.

Leather or Ultrasuede

Leather is frequently used in projects where stones are bezeled onto a backing. Look for supple, split-hide, garment-weight leather. If it's too thick, it will present great difficulty when it comes to stitching the beads in place. (You can always resort to English glover's needles if you have difficulty working with regular beading needles.) Ultrasuede makes a great alternative to leather and is often much easier to stitch through.

Adhesive

E6000 is a great all-purpose adhesive that I use for applying cabochons to leather. I prefer it because not only is it clear, but also once it dries it can be removed from stone surfaces, should you decide to reposition the stone. It does have a strong smell and should be used in a well-ventilated area. If you prefer not to use liquid adhesive, you can also use double-sided carpet tape.

Beads

It goes without saying that there's *no such thing* as too many beads. The range of size, shape, and color is endless. It's nice, over time, to develop a stash to work with when creating your own designs. Having an array to choose from will increase the possibilities and also stimulate your creativity. This section focuses on the material requirements for the book and describes only some of the extensive assortment of beads out there.

Seed Beads

Taking their name from the ancient tradition of drilling holes in seeds to make wearable beads, seed beads today are small glass beads made from pulled rods of glass. They're generally sized in aught sizes, denoted with a slash and a zero, or a degree symbol, as in 15/0 or 15°. The diameter of the bead becomes smaller as the aught number becomes larger. A size 15° bead, for example, is considerably smaller than an 11° bead. **Note:** Generally speaking, Czech beads are smaller than Japanese beads of the same aught size.

15° Czech Charlottes

Charlottes were traditionally Czech size 13° beads with a single facet, creating a glittery appearance. Today the term has been extended to include a wider range of sizes, and even non-Czech beads. Make no mistake—the ones called for in most of the projects in this book are size 15° Czech charlottes, which are considerably smaller than Japanese 15° round beads. Due to their very small size and very small holes, these beads require either a size 13 or a size 15 needle.

Cylinder Beads

Cylinder beads are round cylinder-shaped beads, often called Delicas, Aikos, or Treasures, which are all specific brand names. Unlike other seed beads, they're only lightly fire polished after being cut, and thus retain the shape of the original glass rod. They're wonderful beads to work with; on account of the cylindrical shape, they fit together like tiles and create a very neat appearance in woven beadwork.

Czech Fire-Polished Beads

Czech fire-polished beads are any of a wide range of glass beads that are machine cut and then fire polished to soften the sharp edges and retain the facets. Faceted round beads are the most common shape, although they can also be found in rondelles, faceted rondelles, and faceted teardrop beads.

Pressed Glass Beads

Czech pressed glass beads are made in machines that press the molten glass into a mold. The beads that come out of these molds have rough edges and are often still attached together, so they're broken into individual beads and tumbled to remove the mold edging. Next, the beads are fire polished to soften the edges. Some of the more common pressed glass shapes include drops, daggers, flowers, leaves, and lentils.

German pressed glass beads are made in the same manner, but they're noted for higher quality and greater refinement in detail. Because of higher material and labor costs, they're considerably more expensive than their Czech counterparts.

Crystal Beads

Although Austria is not the only source of crystal beads, it's considered the home of the finest crystal beads. Probably best known is the Swarovski company, located in Wattens, Austria. The high lead content in Swarovski crystal results in a more sparkly glass. In addition to beads, Swarovski also makes crystal gemstones in a large variety of shapes, sizes, and colors. The most commonly used stone is the *rivoli*, a 32-faced round stone pointed on the front and back sides. These stones are excellent for use in beadwork once they've been captured, or encased, in beaded stitching.

Cabochons

A cabochon is a flat-backed, unfaceted gem or stone that's convex in shape and highly polished. It's generally a precious or semiprecious stone, although the term also applies to non-stone materials such as pearls, glass, and even plastic. Cabochons can be calibrated to a set size and form, such as circles, ovals, and squares, or they can be free-form and amorphous.

Gemstone Beads

Gemstone beads are available in a great variety—from common stones all the way up to diamonds. The most important thing to keep in mind when selecting these beads is hole size. Gemstone beads frequently have tiny holes that are nearly impossible to pass through with beading thread even once, yet alone several times. If you plan to incorporate these beads into your embellishments and woven work, make sure the holes allow for it.

Freshwater Pearls

Freshwater pearls are cultured or natural pearls that come from oysters grown in fresh water. Look for good luster, consistency in color, and a large hole size. Pearls with very small holes require the additional tedious job of reaming to make stringing possible.

CHAPTER THREE

BASIC STITCHES AND TECHNIQUES

In off-loom beadwork there are enough different stitches, and variations thereof, to fill an entire book. Rather than attempt to cover all the types of stitching, this chapter is devoted to just the techniques used in the embellishments and projects in this book. Every beaded form you encounter in these pages is constructed using one (or a combination) of the following stitches: peyote stitch, spiral stitch, herringbone stitch, or lacy stitch, and in some cases, bead embroidery and simple stringing techniques.

Peyote Stitch

One of the most useful off-loom stitches is peyote stitch. Its origins aren't entirely certain, but examples of it have been found in artifacts dating as far back as ancient Egypt, as well as in religious objects used by Native Americans for peyote ceremonies. It's likely that the dual existence of the stitch in two entirely different cultures and locations is the result of spontaneous innovation rather than any sort of shared knowledge between the groups.

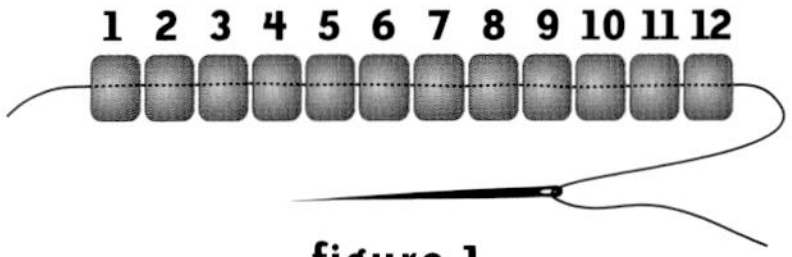

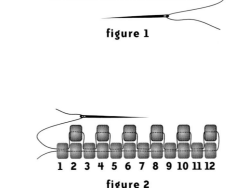

figure 1

figure 2

Flat, Even-Count Peyote Stitch

Flat, even-count peyote stitch is useful when creating a two-dimensional surface to embellish. It's used in several projects in this book, including the Rosebud Bracelet (page 67) and the Cherry Blossom Pendant Necklace (page 86). The weave can be done in a solid, patterned, or randomly mixed color.

To start, string up the number of beads required to create the desired width of the finished piece, tab, or strip. The number of beads can be any even number, from two

beads to hundreds of them, depending on the scale you're working in. Figure 1 shows 12 cylinder beads, although virtually any type of bead can be used for this stitch pattern.

Pick up another—in this case, thirteenth—bead. Stitch back in the opposite direction, passing back through the second-to-last bead in the initial row (#11). Now pick up a new bead, skip over the next bead in the work (#10), and go through the bead after that (#9). Work in this manner until you reach the end of the row (figure 2). You'll

notice that a row of peyote stitch consists of "every other bead," meaning that once you've added this row, the initial strand of 12 has split into 2 rows, resulting in a total of 3 rows, including the row you just stitched. Because of the way beads are added when weaving with peyote stitch, the number of rows stitched is always counted on the diagonal.

To add the next row, weave back in the other direction with the thread, adding 1 bead between every "high bead" in the previous row (figure 3). Continue stitching back and forth in this manner until you've achieved the desired length and size of your beadwork.

To count this stitch, tally the number of beads along one side of the work. Then flip it over and count the number of beads along the other side. Add these two numbers together to get the row count—which depicts 25 rows (figure 4).

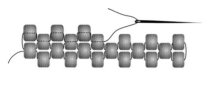

figure 3

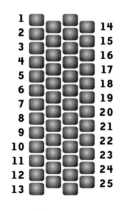

figure 4

Flat, Odd-Count Peyote Stitch

Flat, odd-count peyote stitch is excellent for creating symmetrical geometric patterns within the weave. It can be done using any type of bead, but in this book, flat odd-count peyote stitch is used exclusively with cylinder beads. This stitch is a little more difficult than flat, even-count peyote because the odd number of beads requires a circuitous turnaround to get the thread in position for adding the next row. The turnaround must be done along one side of the strip to lock the last bead of that row in place and position the thread to begin the next row.

To begin, pick up an odd number of beads, illustrated here with 11 beads (figure 5). Pick up another bead, then change the direction of the thread and go back through bead #10. Pick up another new bead and go through bead #8, skipping over the ninth bead in the initial string of beads. Pick up another new bead, skip over #7, and go through #6. Pick up another new bead, skip over #5, and go through #4. Pick up another bead, skip over #3 and go through #2 (figure 6). Pick up another new bead.

Here's where the difference between odd-count and even-count peyote stitch becomes apparent. There's no bead to go through at the end of the row, requiring some manipulation to make the stitch work. To complete the row and make the first turn-around after picking up the last bead, make a U-turn and go back through the last bead in the row below the bead you just picked up—the last bead in the initial row (figure 7). Pick up a bead and go through the next bead along the bottom side of the beadwork. Stitch in this manner

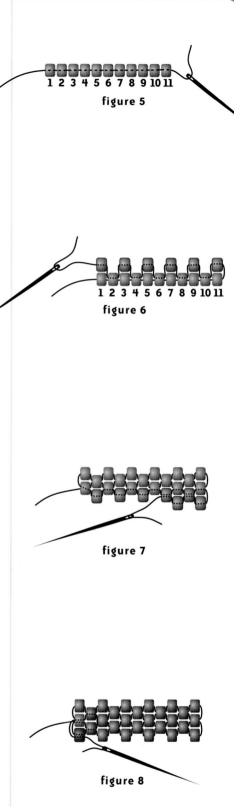

figure 5

figure 6

figure 7

figure 8

and when you reach the far (right-hand) side, do a regular turn around and peyote stitch back in the other direction as shown in figure 7.

Refer to figure 8 as you work this paragraph. To complete the next turn-around after picking up the last bead in this row (shown in green), change direction and go into the bead directly above the bead you are adding (shown in gold). Pass through the bead next to it on an upward diagonal (shown in blue). Change direction and go through the bead directly below the last bead you just passed through (shown in purple). Go up through the yellow bead on a diagonal and then change direction and pass through the end bead on the most recent row (shown in green). You've now completed the turn-around and are ready to peyote stitch back in the other direction.

With flat, odd-count peyote stitch, one side of the strip (the right-hand side in the illustration) always has a straightforward turn around, while the other side (the left-hand side in the illustration) will always require this series of backtracks and U-turns to position the thread properly for the next row.

Tubular, Even-Count Peyote Stitch

Although tubular peyote stitch exists in both even- and odd-count, you only need to know the even-count form for the projects in this book. Tubular, even-count peyote stitch can be used to make thin beaded tubes, which are excellent for neck straps, and can also be applied to building beaded bezels, beaded rings, and other dimensional forms.

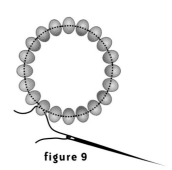

figure 9

To start, string an even number of beads on a single threaded needle; 20 beads are shown in the illustration. Slide the beads down, leaving a 6-inch (15.2 cm) tail, and pass through the first bead again to form a circle of beads (figure 9). Coming out of this first bead in the circle, pick up a new bead, skip over the next bead, and go through the bead after that (figure 10). Continue in this manner until you've worked your way around the initial circle. At the end of this round, you'll *step up*.

figure 10

Step up refers to the thread pass required to bring your working thread up through the last completed row and place it in position to add the next row (figure 11). An easy way to remember the step up is that at the end of each row, you'll have to pass through 2 beads to begin the next row (the last bead in the row you're adding to and the first bead in the row you just completed). It can be difficult to see at first, but from a structural standpoint, step ups are logical because you need to move up a row to continue building (like you would with a circular wall of bricks). Also, keep in mind that the step up "moves" over one space with each new round—*it does not* occur in the same location.

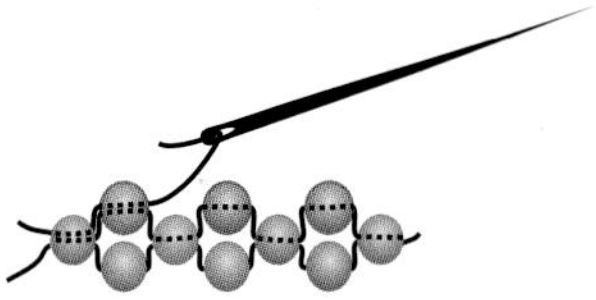

figure 11

figure 12

figure 13

figure 14

Basic Spiral Rope

A tubular form where a series of outer beads spirals around an inner strand of beads, a spiral rope is a derivative of South African beadweaving. It's a beautiful stitch in its own right and provides an excellent base for embellishment. Many variations of this stitch exist. Here, I describe what I consider the basic form, using two colors of size 11° seed beads. I also include a guide to several of the infinite variations.

To build a basic spiral rope using size 11° seed beads, you need two colors of beads, one for the inside or core of the spiral (denoted here as CC, core color), and a second color for the outer portion (signified as OC, outer color). You'll need three times as many of the outer-color beads as core-color beads.

Spiral stitch uses a lot of thread, so work with as much as you can comfortably handle. You'll need to add a new thread several times when working on longer sections of spiral rope. Fortunately, spiral rope stitch works the same in both directions. By beginning in the middle of your working thread, you can work in one direction and then thread up the tail and work in the other direction.

To start, single thread about 2 to 4 wingspans (a wingspan equals about 5 feet [1.5 m]) of beading thread. Wax it well. String on 4 size 11° CC beads and 3 size 11° OC beads. Leave half the thread length as the tail; you'll use it later to work in the opposite direction and it may come in handy for finishing off the end or adding new thread. Pass through the 4 CC beads again to create a circle of beads (figure 12). The

key to success in spiral stitch is maintaining the correct positioning of the beads. Hold the beads in your hand so that the CC beads are to the right and the OC beads are to the left (or vice versa, if you prefer; it's only essential that this positioning remain the same throughout).

After the start stitch, every stitch thereafter is identical: Pick up 1 CC bead and 3 OC beads. Slide all the beads down to the base and count back 4 CC beads (this count includes the one you just added). Pass up through these 4 beads, and fold the new "loop" of OC beads over to the left (figure 13). Always remember to fold this new stitch over; failure to do so will disrupt the spiraling pattern. Continue to stitch until the spiral is the desired length. (If you begin in the middle of your thread when you've completed half the desired length, you can thread up the long tail and stitch the other half to length.)

To add a new thread, weave the tail of the old thread into the spiral, half hitching 2 to 3 times within the outer beads. A new thread is knotted on in the same way. Once attached, weave the new thread through the beads so it's coming out of the last core bead and resume spiral stitch.

Many variations are possible simply by varying the sizes and shapes of the OC beads. Here are bead patterns for a few of my favorite variations. Each uses size 11° seed beads for the core and 4 size 11° CC beads to start. The patterns vary in their choice of OC bead sizes and shapes.

Variation 1
Spiral using 15°–15°–11°–15°–15° as the outer sequence (figure 14).

Variation 2

Spiral using 15°–15°–3-mm maga-tama–15°–15° as the outer sequence (figure 15).

Variation 3

Spiral using 15°–15°–15°–15°–15°–15° as the outer sequence (figure 16).

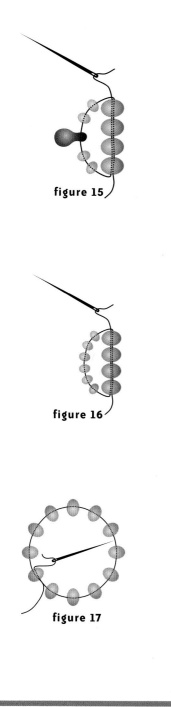

figure 15

figure 16

figure 17

Ndebele or Herringbone

Ndebele, also known as herringbone stitch, originated with the Ndebele tribe of South Africa. It can be worked in both flat and tubular forms, but I use only the tubular form in this book. Tubular Ndebele consists of a sequence of ladders around the perimeter of the tube. Each ladder is 2 beads wide. The beads are positioned next to each other at an angle, creating the appearance of a herringbone pattern. The number of ladders you have around the tube dictates the number of beads you pick up to begin. For every ladder, you need to pick up 4 beads.

Although there are several ways to begin tubular Ndebele, I'll describe the traditional, 3-row start because it can be worked the same from either end, allowing you to seamlessly join 2 separate tubes. In the example shown here, the tube has 3 ladders. Begin by stringing 12 beads (3 ladders times 4 beads per ladder equals 12 beads). Once you've strung your initial count of beads, go back through the first bead to form a circle (figure 17).

Pick up 2 new beads and go through the very next bead (#2). Skip over the next 2 beads (#3 and #4) in the circle and go through the bead after that (#5). Pick up 2 new beads and go through the very next bead (#6). Skip over 2 beads (#7 and #8) in the circle and go through the bead after that (#9). Pick up 2 new beads and go into the very next bead (#10). Skip over the next 2 beads in the circle (#11 and #12) and go through the next bead (#1). Step up through the first bead added; you're ready to begin tubular Ndebele (figure 18).

This traditional start can be a little tricky when you first learn it, but the benefits far outweigh the disadvantages. When you pull on your thread, the beads should shift into place and form the 3 ladders (figure 19). Once the base is formed, every row is the same. The thread will exit one of the beads in one of the ladders: pick up 2 beads and go down into the second bead in that ladder. Do a U-turn and come up through the first bead in the next ladder, pick up 2 beads, and go back down the second bead in this second ladder (figure 20, shown in two dimensions).   *Continued on next page.*

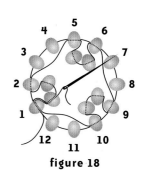

figure 18

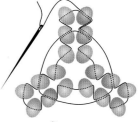

figure 19

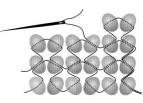

figure 20

Continue all the way around until you get back to the first ladder. Just as in tubular, even-count peyote, you'll have a step up at the end of each row. If you forget to step up, your ladders will start spiraling rather than continuing on straight.

Lacy Stitch

Lacy stitch, also know as netting, is a more open-weave variation of peyote stitch and has been popular throughout history, especially during the Victorian era. Netting has been used on clothing, in jewelry, and as an embellishment on accessories such as purses and scarves. As with peyote, lacy stitch can be worked in both flat and tubular forms. For the projects in this book, only the tubular form is used.

To begin, string up a sequence of beads. This can vary greatly depending on the openness of the weave and the size of the beads. The directions provided here are intended only as an illustration of the basic weave rather than a precise stitching format. For example, the sequence could be: A–B–B–C–B–B–A–B–B–C–B–B–A–B–B–C–B–B–A–B–B–C–B–B.

Circle around and pass through the first A bead a second time to create a circle of beads (figure 21). Pick up B–B–C–B–B and go through the next A bead. Repeat 3 more times until you reach the original A bead (figure 22). Now you're ready to step down—to weave down to the next level to begin another round of beads.

In the example here, after passing through the original A bead, pass through the B–B–C beads in the second round (figure 23). To begin a third round, pick up B–B–A–B–B and go through the next C bead. Repeat 3 more times until you reach the C bead where you began the row. Step down, passing through B–B–A to begin the next round (figure 24). Continue in this manner for the desired length, with the A and C beads serving as high and low beads would in peyote stitch.

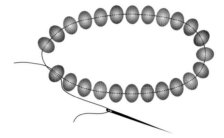

figure 21

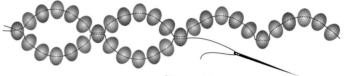

figure 22

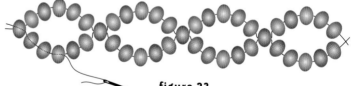

figure 23

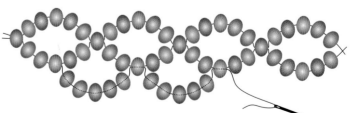

figure 24

Some Basic Forms

Ring forms are useful for all sorts of bead construction, most notably as toggle rings. These directions give you the basic form; it's solid but self-supporting, with no internal armature.

Ring Form

The basic ring form is created using size 15° Japanese round seed beads and size 11° Japanese cylinder beads.

Step 1: Thread approximately 5 feet (1.5 m) of 6-lb. FireLine on a size 13 English beading needle. Wax well. Thread on 36 size 15° Japanese seed beads and pass again through the first bead to create a circle. Don't tie a knot. Leave a 6-inch (15.2 cm) tail (figure 25).

Step 2: Begin peyote stitching with 15°s. Complete 1 round and step up (figure 26).

Step 3: For the next round of peyote stitch, use size 11° cylinder beads. At the end of this round, step up (figure 27).

Step 4: Do another round of peyote stitch using 11° cylinder beads. At the end of this round, step up (figure 28).

Step 5: Do another round of peyote stitch with 11° cylinder beads, and then weave through the beads to the other side of the 15°s (figure 29).

Step 6: Do 1 round of peyote stitch with 11° cylinder beads. At the end of this round, step up (figure 30).

Step 7: Do another round of peyote stitch with 11° cylinder beads. At the end of this round, step up (figure 31).

Step 8: Zip the 2 sides together to create a solid ring. After completing the zip-up, you may want to put a half hitch in between the beads to hold everything tight. If you're using this ring form to make a toggle closure, this working thread will be used later to make a connector tab—in which case, don't weave it off. If you plan only to use the ring form, half hitch 2 or 3 times and weave off the thread. You can also weave off the tail thread (figure 32).

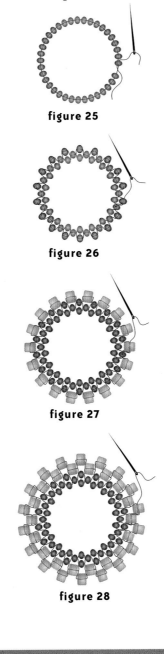

figure 25

figure 26

figure 27

figure 28

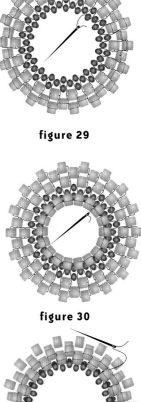

figure 29

figure 30

figure 31

figure 32

23

Peyote Tube Bead

Simple beaded beads can be constructed using basic flat peyote stitch (even- or odd-count). Peyote stitch a strip that is at least 12 rows long (count 6 up either side) and as narrow or as wide as you desire. Roll the strip onto itself and zip the last row to the first row to create a tube, as shown in figure 33. Leave the tube as is or embellish its surface to add a layer of dimension and visual interest.

Toggle Closure

Metal closures on elaborately beaded jewelry often create a sense of disharmony. By utilizing both the ring form and the peyote tube bead form, you can create a beautiful toggle closure entirely out of beads that maintains visual consistency with the overall piece. This toggle closure is created using size 15° and 11° seed beads and size 11° cylinder beads.

Toggle Loop

Step 1: Refer to figure 34. Stitch a ring form to be used for the ring portion of the toggle loop. Follow the ring form directions on page 23.

Step 2: Add on a peyote-stitched tab. Make sure your thread is exiting from the middle row of cylinder beads in the ring. Pick up 1 cylinder bead and go through the next cylinder bead in the center row. This newly added bead will sit between the high beads of the center row on the outside of the ring (figure 35). Pick up a new cylinder bead, change thread direction, and go back through the first bead added (figure 36). Peyote stitch back and forth to create a flat strip of even-count peyote 2 beads wide by 16 rows long (count 8 beads up either

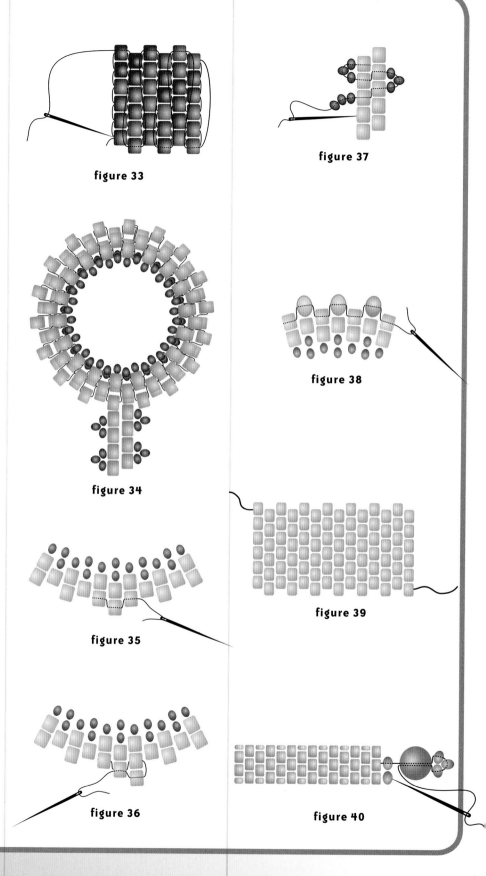

figure 33

figure 37

figure 34

figure 38

figure 35

figure 39

figure 36

figure 40

24

side). Zip the last row to the first row of the tab to create a *connector loop*.

Finish off the connector loop by embellishing each side with picots of 15°s (or you can use 15° Czech charlottes). A picot (or "small point") is formed by coming out of a bead, picking up 3 beads, and going into the same bead or the next bead, depending on the nature of the picot. In this case, come out of a cylinder bead, pick up three 15°s and go into the bead next to it. Then change thread direction and come out of the next bead (figure 37). Repeat the process.

Step 3: Add one 11° seed bead between every cylinder bead in the center outer row of the toggle loop to create an additional design detail (figure 38).

Toggle Bar

Step 4: Refer to figure 39. Pick up 14 cylinder beads to begin a strip of flat, even-count peyote stitch 14 beads wide by 12 rows long (count 6 beads up either side). Once the strip's complete, zip the first row to the last row to form a tube.

Step 5: Add a bead embellishment to both ends of the tube (figure 40). It's attached to the ends of the tube in the following manner: Coming out of one of the cylinder beads at one end of the tube, pick up one 15°, the bead, and 3 more 15°s. Pass back through the bead, pick up a 15°, and go into the second cylinder bead at the end of the tube. Do a U-turn within the peyote stitch of the tube and come back up out of the third cylinder bead at the end of the tube. Pick up one 15°, go up through the bead, and pass through the three 15°s in the picot formed previously. Go back down through the bead and pick up 1 more 15°. Go down through the fourth cylinder bead

around the end of the tube. Repeat this process 1 more time. By using a 15° above each end cylinder bead in the tube and beneath the bead, the bead is centered over the end of the tube. Weave the working thread to the other end of the tube and repeat the process.

Step 6: Using either your tail thread or your working thread, weave to the center beads of the tube (seventh and eighth column of the 14 beads across). Coming out of the sixth column, pick up 1 cylinder bead and go through the next bead in that row (in the eighth column), as shown in figure 41. Turn around, pick up another cylinder bead, and come back through the cylinder bead you previously added. Weave back and forth in this manner, creating a strip of flat, even-count peyote that is 2 beads wide by 16 rows long (count 8 beads up each side), as shown in figure 42.

Once the tab is the correct length, zip the last row of the tab to the first row of the tab to create a connector loop and embellish the edges of the tab with 15° picots (or you can use 15° Czech charlottes for the picots).

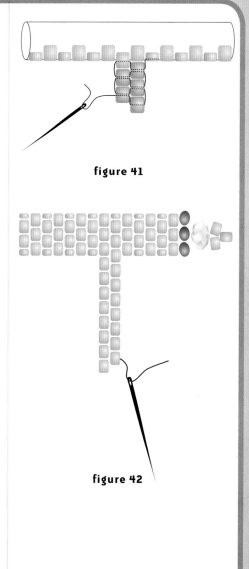

figure 41

figure 42

25

CHAPTER FOUR
A COMPREHENSIVE GUIDE TO EMBELLISHMENTS

This chapter provides you with the basic directions for a large variety of organically inspired embellishment forms. Beginning with simpler forms and working through to more complex structures, I'll lead you, step by step, through the three-dimensional construction of these useful embellishments. Later on in the projects chapter, you'll see how each of these forms can be applied and combined with other forms to make lavishly embellished jewelry.

Simple Embellishments

The simple embellishments shown in the figures can create an endless array of dimensional forms; simply clustering some, as shown in the photographs, can make a lot of impact. These are formed by means of simple stringing, and require no weaving, per se.

figure 1

figure 2

Simple Bud

This is the most basic of the simple embellishments and forms the basis for many other simple and complex embellishments. The bud is formed by coming out of a bead or textile surface, picking up one 11°, 1 accent bead (this can be any type of center-drilled bead—a pearl, a Czech glass bead, a gemstone bead, etc.), and three 15°s. Pass back through the center-drilled bead, the 11°, and go back into the bead or textile surface from which you originally emerged. The 3 size 15°s form a picot at the top of the bud form (figure 1)

Simple Flower

The simple flower form is an extension of the basic bud form. It's formed by coming out of the bead or textile surface, picking up one 11°, 1 rondelle, 1 center-drilled glass flower bead, 1 pearl (or other type of center-drilled bead), and three 15°s. Weave back down through the pearl, the flower, the rondelle, the 11°, and back into the bead or textile surface. There are many ways to vary the form, including longer stems, a beaded pistil that extends from the pearl to the picot, and a multitude of branching options (figure 2).

Simple Leaf

A simple leaf refers to an embellishment constructed using a leaf-shaped bead, rather than a beaded leaf form. (The beaded leaf is explained in the basic floral embellishments and advanced floral embellishments sections on pages 31 and 41.) There are two basic types of leaf-shaped beads. One is center drilled from top to bottom, while the other is top drilled from side to side on the stem end of the leaf. They're handled differently when attaching them to a beaded form, but both types are equally effective in creating the image of a leaf.

The center-drilled leaf is added by coming out of the bead or textile surface, picking up one 11°, 1 glass leaf bead, and three 15°s, and weaving back down through the leaf, the 11°, and back into the bead or textile surface (figure 3).

The top-drilled leaf is added by coming out of the bead or textile surface, picking up one 11°, five 15°s, 1 glass leaf bead, and 5 more 15°s, and weaving back through the 11° and back into the bead or textile surface. This means of embellishing uses the 15°s to cover thread that would otherwise show if you were adding just the leaf bead (figure 4).

Simple Drop

These are exceptionally useful elements and when used in multiples can mimic the forms of bubbles or berries, depending on your intention. They come in a large variety of sizes and are made both in the Czech Republic and in Japan. The Japanese drop beads are often referred to as *magatamas* or *fringe beads*. Simple drops, regardless of size, are added in the same manner.

Coming out of a bead or textile surface, pick up one 11° and anywhere from two to five 15°s (this count depends on the size of the drop—3-mm magatamas usually only require two 15°s, 4 x 6-mm drops require three or four 15°s, and larger drops may require even more). Pick up the drop bead and the same number of 15°s as picked up earlier. Go back through the 11° and into the bead or textile surface. The 15°s used on either side of the drop will cover the thread (figure 5).

figure 3

figure 4

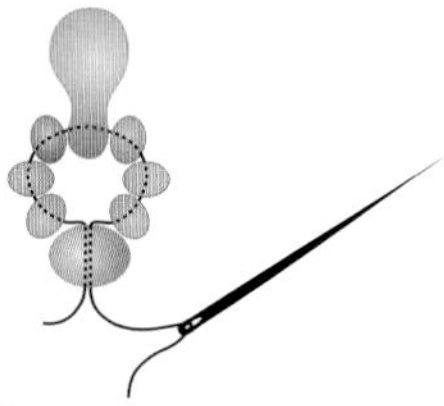

figure 5

Simple Dagger

Dagger beads are basically a pointed variation on the drop beads discussed in the previous section. They're generally produced in the Czech Republic, and like the drops, come in a wide range of sizes. Because they're similar in form, daggers are added on in the same manner as drops. Coming out of a bead or textile surface, pick up one 11°, anywhere from 3 to 5 size 15°s (depending on the size of the dagger), the dagger itself, and again 3 to 5 size 15°s. Go back through the 11° and into the bead or textile surface (figure 6).

figure 6

Basic Floral Embellishments

These forms are made by compounding the previously described simple embellishments. They often take longer to construct, but because they're more elaborate they convey a more realistic representation of floral forms.

Flower Cluster

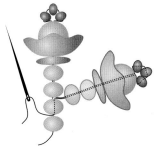

A flower cluster is a variation of the simple flower described on page 27. Rather than just a single flower, it has branches, each ending in a flower form. There are many possibilities for this basic flower form, including longer stems, a beaded pistil extending from the pearl to the picot, and a large range of branching options.

Coming out of the bead or textile surface, pick up—for example—four 11°s, 1 rondelle, 1 center-drilled glass flower bead, 1 pearl (or other type of center-drilled bead), and three 15°s. Go back down through the pearl, the flower, the rondelle, and the next two 11°s (figure 7). Coming out between the second and third 11°, pick up two 11°s, 1 rondelle, 1 center-drilled glass flower bead, 1 pearl, and three 15°s. Go back down through the pearl, flower, rondelle, and two 11°s, and down through the next 11° in the stalk of the branch (figure 8). Exiting the 11° bead, pick up 2 new 11°s, 1 rondelle, 1 center-drilled glass flower bead, 1 pearl, and three 15°s. Go back down through the pearl, flower, rondelle, and two 11°s, and down through the last 11° in the stalk of the branch and back into the bead or textile surface (figure 9).

figure 7

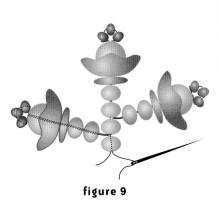

figure 8

figure 9

Berry Cluster

This is a simple but fantastic form for creating dimension and volume in botanical (as well as oceanic) inspired beadwork. Cluster forms build up volume relatively quickly while maintaining a delicate overall look. Berry clusters can be made from a variety of bead sizes, but I generally use 15° seed beads, 11° seed beads, and 3-mm magatamas and/or 4 x 6-mm Czech drop beads. The number of 11°s used in the stalk determines the number of drops, or "berries." If you begin with five 11°s, you'll end up with 5 drops (or berries).

Coming out of a bead or textile surface, pick up 5 size 11° seed beads, 3 size 15° seed beads, 1 drop/magatama, and 3 more 15°s. Go back up through the last (fifth) 11° and pull the beads tight (figure 10). You have completed 1 berry. To start the second, pick up 3 size 15°s, 1 drop/magatama, and 3 more 15°s. Go back up through the next (fourth) 11° (figure 11). Pull tight. Repeat 3 more times, adding the three 15°s, drop/magatama, and three 15°s between each 11° (see figures 12, 13, and 14). Once you reach the top and have passed through the first 11°, sew back into the bead or textile surface.

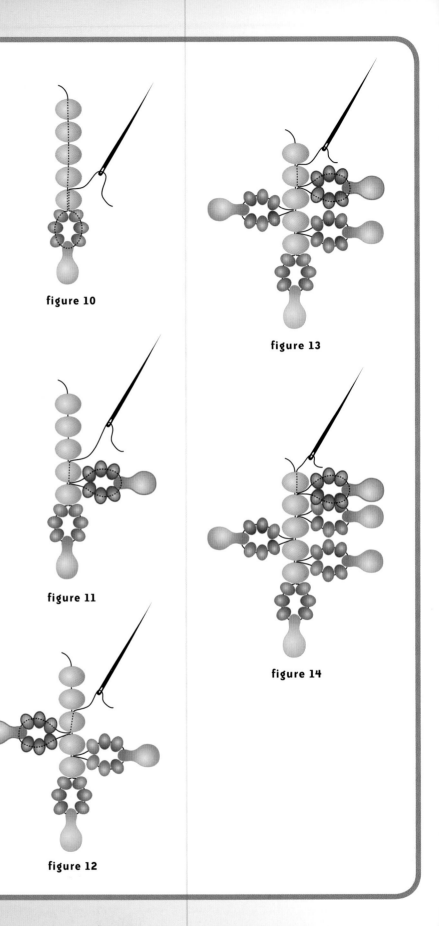

figure 10

figure 11

figure 12

figure 13

figure 14

Basic Beaded Leaf

Infinite variations of beaded leaves can be made using seed beads. A great basic version is this strung (versus woven) form. It's a quick and effective method of creating leaflike forms. These basic leaves can be made from any number of bead shapes and sizes. The one described here uses size 11° and size 15° seed beads.

Coming out of the bead or textile surface, pick up one 11° seed bead, five 15° seed beads, one 11° seed bead, and three 15° seed beads. (Colors can vary or remain the same throughout, as you wish.) Go back through the most recently strung 11° to create a picot of the three 15°s (figure 15). Pick up 5 new 15°s and go back through the 11° at the base of the form and sew back into the bead or textile surface (figure 16). By varying the number of beads strung up between the 11°s (in this case it was 5), you can change the overall length of the leaf.

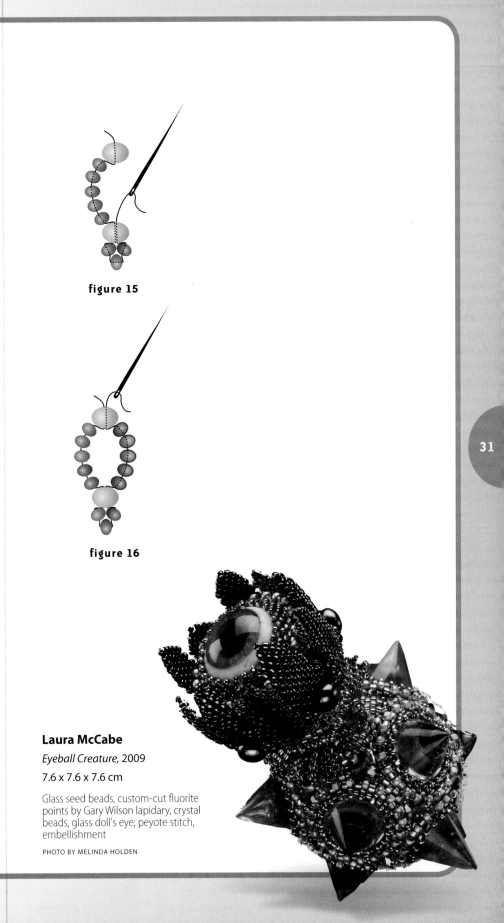

figure 15

figure 16

31

Laura McCabe

Eyeball Creature, 2009

7.6 x 7.6 x 7.6 cm

Glass seed beads, custom-cut fluorite points by Gary Wilson lapidary, crystal beads, glass doll's eye; peyote stitch, embellishment

PHOTO BY MELINDA HOLDEN

Frond Form

This form's shape reminds me of fern fronds, hence the name. In addition to looking good with floral forms, it works well as a sea-inspired embellishment.

Although it can be made from a large variety of bead shapes and sizes, the example here is constructed using 11° and 15° seed beads and a 2 x 4-mm glass rondelle.

Coming out of the bead or textile surface, string up 12 (or any even number) 11° seed beads, 1 rondelle, and three 15° seed beads. Go back through the rondelle to create a picot of 15°s and pull the beads down tight against the form out of which the embellishment is being built. String up an 11° seed bead, skip over the 11° directly next to the rondelle, and go through the next 11° after that. Continue peyote stitching in this manner until you reach the base of the frond form). After going through the first 11°, weave back into the bead or textile surface. Due to the tension created by pulling the initial strand of beads tight up against the base bead or textile, a natural curve will form (figures 18 and 19).

figure 18

figure 19

Advanced Floral Embellishments

Advanced floral embellishments include a vast range of floral forms that employ one or more beadweaving techniques to create three-dimensional forms. They're considerably more elaborate than the simple embellishments and basic floral embellishments and take much more time to complete. However, they add a whole different dimension of detail and form.

Star Flower

The star flower is a delightful form that utilizes peyote stitch sewn around a pearl center to create a pretty beaded flower. It resembles a beautiful snowflake when beaded in silver or white.

String any amount of 11° seed beads (for example, 4), one 4-mm freshwater pearl, and three 15°s (in A–B–A color sequence). Go back through the pearl to create a picot of the 15°s (figure 20).

Pick up seven 15°s (in B–A–B–A–B–A–B color sequence). Go through all 3 beads in the picot, then pick up 7 more 15°s (in B–A–B–A–B–A–B color sequence). Pass through the bottommost 11° (on the stalk) toward the pearl. This will cause the 11° to rotate sideways against the pearl (figure 21).

figure 20

figure 21

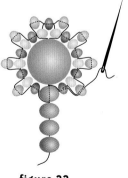

figure 22

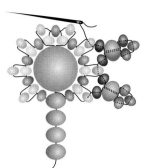

figure 23

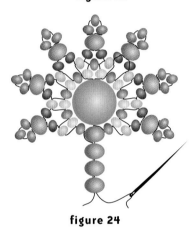

figure 24

Go through the first 15° in the circle of beads around the pearl (a B-colored bead). Begin peyote stitching with C-colored 15°s. When you reach the picot, pass through just the middle bead, and continue peyote stitching along the other side. When you reach the stalk, pass through the bottommost 11° toward the pearl and step up through a B bead from the first round and the C bead from the last round (figure 22). You're ready to add petals between each of the C beads.

Coming out of the first C bead, pick up one 15° (D color), one 11°, and three 15°s (E color). Go back through the 11° to form a picot of E-colored 15°s. Pick up a D-colored

15° and go through the next C bead (figure 23). Repeat this process 6 more times, creating a total of 7 petals. Once you've gone though the last C bead (finishing the seventh petal), pass through the 15° (B color) and down through the second 11° (from the pearl) in the stalk. The 11° in the stalk that's against the pearl has been totally incorporated into the flower form so you won't need to pass through it (figure 24).

Pointed Peyote Petals

Peyote petals add fantastic detail to floral forms. This basic petal shape can be used individually or in multiples to create flower forms.

Thread up 3 feet (91.4 cm) of single thread and wax well. Pick up nine 15°s, and slide the beads down, leaving 12 inches (30.5 cm) of tail. Go back through the sixth 15° to create a picot out of the last 3 beads. Peyote stitch back toward the first bead (the base of the petal) using 15°s. When you reach the base of the petal, do a U-turn and come up through the first bead. You've completed the central vein of the petal and are now set for another round (figure 25). *Continued on next page.*

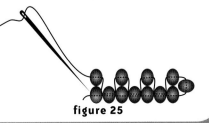

figure 25

figure 26

figure 27

figure 28

Stitch another round of peyote, making sure you pass through all 3 beads in the picot to maintain the pointed shape of the petal tip (figure 26). Do a U-turn and step up through 2 beads before resuming peyote. Peyote stitch, adding 2 beads—1 at a time—then pass through all 5 beads in the petal tip before resuming peyote and adding 2 beads—again, 1 at a time—on the other side (figure 27). When you reach the petal base, do a final U-turn and step up through 3 beads along the petal edge. Add 1 bead and then pass through 7 beads in the petal tip. Add another bead on the other side of the petal and then step down through 3 beads so you emerge at the petal base (figure 28).

Rounded Peyote Petals

As with the pointed peyote petals, the rounded variation is constructed by peyote stitching around a central strip of peyote stitch. Using additional 15°s at the rounded end of the petal in this variation creates a slightly curved petal form that accurately mimics real-life petals.

Thread a size 13 English beading needle with 3 feet (91.4 cm) of single thread, then pick up 9 size 15° seed beads. Go back through the sixth seed bead to form a picot of the last 3 beads strung up. Peyote stitch down to the base of the petal form (figure 29).

Make a U-turn and go back through the first seed bead. Pick up a new bead and go through the third original seed bead. Continue peyote stitching around the petal in this manner until you've returned

figure 29

figure 30

figure 31

figure 32

figure 33

to the petal base (figure 30). Note that at the picot, you pick up a bead on either side of the middle picot bead to maintain a rounded shape.

Again make a U-turn and step up through two 15°s, bringing you to the outer edge of the form, before resuming peyote stitch. This ensures a tapered shape at the base of the petal. Continue peyote stitching to fill in the outer edge along this side of the petal. Pass through the three 15°s on the rounded end of the petal and resume peyote stitching, adding three 15°s to this edge of the flower petal. Step down, passing through two 15°s and emerging at the base of the petal (figure 31).

This time, step up through three 15°s to get to the outer edge of the petal. Resume peyote stitch, adding two 15°s to the outer edge of the petal. Pass through five 15°s on the round end of the petal. Resume peyote stitching, adding two 15°s to this side of the flower petal. Step down, passing through three 15°s to the base of the petal (figure 32).

For the final round, step up through 4 beads, add a bead, and step down and sew through the perimeter beads to the opposite side of the petal. Peyote stitch 1 bead and sew through 4 more perimeter beads to emerge at the base of the leaf (figure 33).

Petals can be constructed individually and then attached, or they can be linked to create a flower form (see the directions for the Cherry Blossom embellishment on page 38).

Laura McCabe

Agate Face Necklace, 2008

Pendant, 5.1 x 8.9 cm

Rare agate carved face by Gary Wilson, glass seed beads, freshwater pearls, Japanese keshi pearls, mink fur, leather; embroidery, peyote stitch, flat spiral, embellishment

PHOTO BY MELINDA HOLDEN

Lacy Stitch Rosebud

These delicate little forms, constructed in circular lacy stitch, are derived from Victorian-era beaded flowers that were both used in jewelry and stitched to garments. In this variation, once the petals are complete, the flower is pulled in on the back side to create a ball shape, which may later be added to bead or textile surfaces.

Create the Base

Initial Base Ring: Thread up approximately 6 feet (1.8 m) of thread onto a size 13 English beading needle. Pick up four 15° seed beads and knot a circle, leaving about 6 inches (15 cm) of tail thread. This forms the initial base ring. Go through one of the four 15°s to hide the knot (figure 34).

Base Round 1 (adding 3 beads each time): Pick up three 15°s and go through the next 15° in the initial base ring (figure 35). Repeat this process all the way around until there are 4 sets of 3 beads worked off of the initial base ring (figure 36).

Base Round 2 (adding 5 beads each time): Step up through 2 beads, so you're coming out of the middle bead on the first set of 3 (as shown in figure 36). Pick up five 15°s and go through the middle bead on the next set of 3. Repeat this all the way around until you have 4 sets of 5 beads (figure 37).

Base Round 3 (adding 7 beads each time): Step up through 3 beads, so you're coming out of the middle (third) bead on the first set of 5. Pick up seven 15°s and go through the middle bead on the next set of 5.

Repeat this all the way around until you have 4 sets of 7 beads (figure 38).

Base Round 4 (adding 9 beads each time): Step up through 4 beads, so you're coming out of the middle (fourth) bead on the first set of 7. Pick up nine 15°s and go through the middle bead on the next set of 7. Repeat this all the way around until you have 4 sets of 9 beads (figure 39).

Add the Rose Montée

Weave your thread to the center of the base so you're coming out of one of the 4 beads in the Initial Base Ring. Using your working thread, pick up 1 rose montée (size 12ss or 13ss). Be sure to position the montée right side up on the bead base. Utilizing the two channels on the back side of the montée, make a figure eight by going through the bead directly opposite the bead you're first coming out of, passing back through the montée, and going back through the first bead (figure 40). Once the montée is attached, you're ready to begin the flower petals.

Make the Flower Petals

Note: In the illustrations, base beads are indicated by a red ring around each bead. Only relevant base beads are shown, although the entire base is complete.

Petal Row 1: Coming out of one of the four 15°s in the Initial Base Ring, pick up 3 size 15° Czech charlottes. Go back into the next 15° in the base ring. Repeat 3 more times to make 4 small petals directly against the montée (figure 41).

Petal Row 2: Step up so you're coming out of the first of 3 beads in Base Round 1. Pick up three 15°s and pass through the third of the 3 beads in Base Round 1. Pass through the 15° in the initial circle, then repeat 3 more times to create 4 slightly larger petals

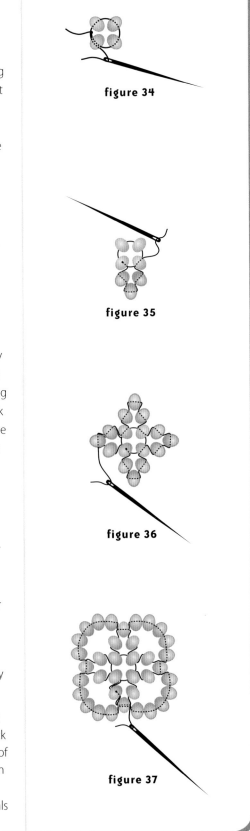

figure 34

figure 35

figure 36

figure 37

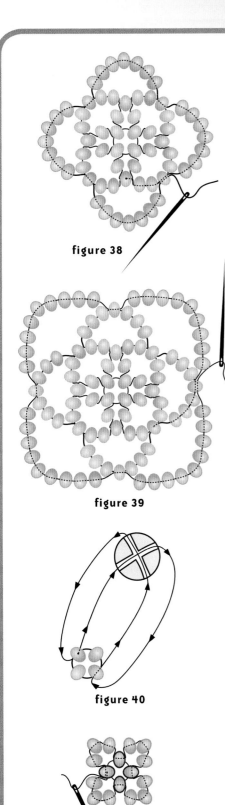

figure 38

figure 39

figure 40

figure 41

that are pressed against the previous row of petals (figure 42).

Petal Row 3: Step up so you're coming out of the second of 3 beads in Base Round 1. Pick up five 15° seed beads and go through the second of 3 beads in the next set in Base Round 1. Repeat 3 more times so there are 4 slightly larger petals pressed against the previous row of petals (figure 43).

Petal Row 4: Step up so you're coming out of the first of 5 beads in Base Round 2. Pick up seven 15° seed beads and go through the fifth of 5 beads in the same set in Base Round 2, then go through the second of 3 beads in the next set in Base Round 1. Repeat 3 more times so there are 4 slightly larger petals pressed against the previous row of petals (figure 44).

Petal Row 5: Step up so you're coming out of the third of 5 beads in Base Round 2. Pick up seven 15° seed beads and go through the third of 5 beads in the next set in Base Round 2. Repeat 3 more times so there are 4 same-sized petals offset from those made in previous row (figure 45).

Petal Row 6: Step up so you're coming out of the first of 7 beads in Base Round 3. Pick up nine 15° seed beads and go through the seventh of 7 beads in the same set in Base Round 3, then go through the third of 5 beads in the next set in Base Round 2. Repeat 3 more times so there are 4 slightly larger petals pressed against the previous row of petals (figure 46).

Petal Row 7: Step up so you're coming out of the fourth of 7 beads in Base Round 3. Pick up nine 15° seed beads and sew through the fourth of 7 beads in the next set in Base Round 3. Repeat 3 more times so there are 4 same-sized petals offset from those made in previous row (figure 47).
Continued on next page.

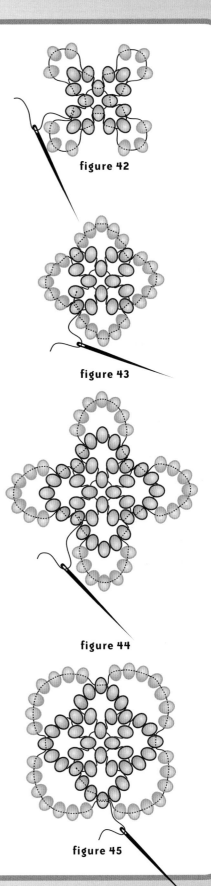

figure 42

figure 43

figure 44

figure 45

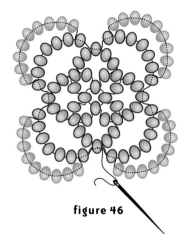

figure 46

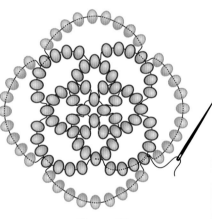

figure 47

Pull in the Back Side

Before pulling in the back side of the flower to create the ball form, you need to weave in the tail created at the beginning of the rosebud.

The tail should be coming out of one of the 4 beads in the Initial Base Ring. Weave up to the top side of the flower and half hitch the thread twice within the petals before cutting the tail. With your working thread, weave your needle through the base so you're coming out of the fifth of 9 beads in one of the sections in Base Round 4. Pick up an 11° and sew through the fifth of the 9 beads in the next section in Base Round 4. Repeat 3 more times so there's one 11° between each of the fifth beads in each section of Base Round 4. Pull tight and the back side of the flower will pull in to form a ball (figure 48). Pass through the circle of 11°s and 15°s a couple more times to strengthen this tightening, then half hitch 2 or 3 times within the petals before cutting off the tails.

To better understand how these rosebuds can be attached to beadwork or textile surfaces, see the Rosebud Ring (page 64) or the Rosebud Bracelet (page 67).

Cherry Blossom

These beautiful beaded flowers are inspired by the exquisite little blossoms that predominate Japanese artwork, textiles, and paper. They're constructed by linking 5 of the rounded peyote-stitched petals described on page 34. By linking the petals as they're woven, you create a stable flower form in which the petals don't flop around but instead stay in place.

Using approximately 8 feet (2.4 m) of single thread on a size 13 beading needle, follow the directions on page 34 to create a single rounded peyote petal. After creating the first petal, move on to the next: Without cutting your thread, add 1 "between petals" 15° and then create the second petal in the same manner as the first, so they're attached. As you stitch the second through the fifth petals, a connection along the lower portion of the petal must be made to help preserve the correct form. The connection is accomplished as you begin round 3 of peyote in the second petal. Step up through 3 beads in the petal, then change directions and go down through the corresponding 3 beads in the previous petal. Pass through the "between petals" 15°. Step up again through the 3 beads in the petal and resume the normal procedure of peyote, stitching round 3 of the petal you're working on. By attaching each petal to the previous one in this manner, the flower retains a better form (figure 49).

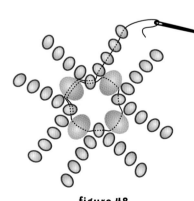

figure 48

38

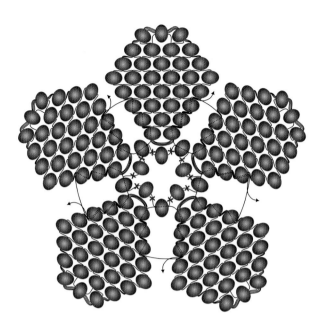

figure 49

Once all 5 petals are complete, you need to add 1 bead between each of the "between petals" 15°s that were added in the petal-connecting process. Using peyote stitch, add a total of five 15° beads to establish 10 beads around the inside of the petal as shown in figure 49.

The stamens are added between each of these ten 15°s. Coming out of one of the 15°s, pick up four 15° Czech charlottes and one 11° seed bead. Go back down through the charlottes and into the next bead in the center of the flower (figure 50). The 11° serves as an end bead to hold the stem in place. Ultimately, you'll add 10 stamens before weaving in and cutting off the tail threads. Figure 49 indicates with an X where to place each of the stamens.

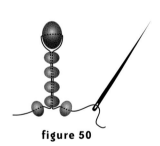

figure 50

The cherry blossom forms are then attached to a larger piece of beadwork by using a pearl and a picot to tack down the embellishment. For more details on this attachment technique, see the directions for the Cherry Blossom Pendant Necklace (page 86).

Pokeweed

Pokeweed, also know as ink berries, is a plant native to my home state of Connecticut. Although generally considered a weed, this plant is exquisite in both form and color (see a photo of it on page 52) and has served as great inspiration in many of my beaded works. The berries in this form are made using pearls, added as embellishments between the core beads on a spiral rope.

Weave a section of spiral rope (page 20). Any variation of spiral will work, but I usually opt for the one that uses 11°s as core beads and two 15°s–one 11°–two 15°s for the outer sequence (see diagram on page 20). Once the spiral is the desired length for the pokeweed cluster, continue by adding an end berry.
Continued on next page.

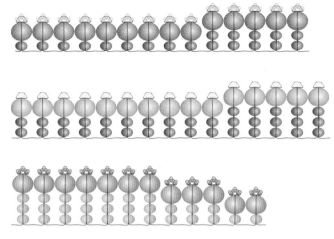

figure 51

Add the End Berry

Using the tail thread at the end of your spiral rope, pick up 1 small pearl (3–4 mm), and three 15°s. Double back through the pearl and go down through 3 core beads. Pick up two 15°s, one 11°, and one 15°, go back through the pearl and the picot, pass back through the pearl again, then go down through 2 core beads. Pick up two 15°s and one 11°. You probably won't be able to fit through the pearl again, so just go back down through the first core bead, skipping the pearl and picot. Finally, pick up two 15°s and go down through the first core bead again. Tie off and weave in your tail thread.

Add the Other Berries

Double thread about 60 inches (152.4 cm) of thread and wax it well. Weave it in, knotting on several times, and work your way up to the tip, so you're coming out between the first and second core beads (right after where you added

the end berry). Begin embellishing with 3- to 4-mm pearls; add one 11°, the pearl, and three 15°s (to create a picot) and pass back through the pearl, the 11°, and the next core bead. Continue to add a pearl in this manner between every core bead, following the diagram from left to right, top to bottom (figure 51; the first small pearl you've already added isn't shown).

Increase the number of 11°s as you move up the stem. After adding the desired number of 3- to 4-mm pearls, add medium-size pearls (5–6 mm), and finally large ones (6–8 mm). The counts shown in the diagram are merely a suggestion in terms of pearl counts.

As you approach the top of your berry cluster, transition back down to two 11°s, and then one 11° underneath the pearls (as shown in the diagram) to bring in the shape of the berry cluster.

Basic Peyote Leaf

There are infinite variations of peyote-stitched leaf forms, but this is a good basic form that can be used as the foundation for more elaborate leaves, such as grape leaves, described later. Peyote leaves are made using cylinder beads and 15°s, woven into flat peyote.

String on an even number (for example, 12) of 11° cylinder beads in color A (center vein color) and three 15°s. Double back through the twelfth cylinder bead to create a picot of the 15°s. Pick up another cylinder bead (color A), skip over 1 bead, and go through the tenth cylinder bead. Continue peyote stitching in this manner until you get to the first cylinder bead strung on. When you get to the end, there will be 1 more cylinder bead on the strand (the first 1 you strung up). Pick up another A-colored cylinder bead, turn around, and go up through the first cylinder bead (figure 52). Continue peyote stitching another row around the vein of the leaf. At this point, switch over to a different color of size 11° cylinder beads (color B). Peyote stitch until you get to the tip (picot) of the leaf. Add a 15° instead of a cylinder bead and go through the picot, and again add a 15° on the other side of the picot—this will give the tip of the leaf a nice curved dimensionality (figure 53). Continue peyote stitching around the central vein 1 more time, until the leaf is the desired width. Weave in and knot off the working thread and the tail thread (figure 54).

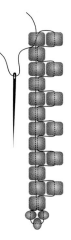

figure 52

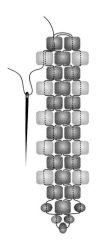

figure 53

figure 54

Peyote Grape Leaf

Peyote grape leaves are a more advanced variation of the basic peyote leaf with three lobes. They're not only great as grapes leaves, but they also can realistically represent the leaves of a large variety of plants, including passionflower and poplar. They're constructed using 11° cylinder beads and 15°s, and as with the basic peyote leaf, can be made using two colors of cylinder beads to suggest a center vein.

String up 12 cylinder beads in color A (center vein color) and three 15°s. Go back through the last cylinder bead to form a picot and peyote stitch with cylinder beads (color A) toward the base of the leaf.

When you get to the bottom of the leaf, pick up 1 more cylinder bead, do a U-turn, and pass back up through the first cylinder bead (figure 55).

You're set to stitch another round of peyote. Do it in the same manner, using color B cylinder beads. When you approach the tip of the petal, go through all three 15°s in the picot and peyote stitch down the other side toward the base of the leaf.

At the base of the leaf, make a U-turn and step up through 2 beads. Do a second round of peyote stitch with cylinder beads, maintaining the point at the tip of the leaf by passing through all 3 beads in the picot as well as the cylinder beads on either side

figure 55

figure 56

41

of the picot (figure 56).

When you get to the bottom of the leaf after the second round of cylinder beads, turn around as before and step up through 3 beads. Begin another round of peyote stitching with cylinder beads. This time add only 2 cylinder beads, then pick up a bead and do a U-turn and stitch through the previously added bead. Peyote stitch 1 bead, then do a U-turn and pass through the previously added bead (figure 57). Peyote stitch 1 bead. Pick up a cylinder bead and do a U-turn and pass through the previously added bead. Make a U-turn and pass through the last cylinder bead you added. Pick up 3 size 15° beads, do a U-turn, and go up through the adjacent cylinder bead, forming a picot (figure 58).

Once the first lobe is complete with picot, weave back to the base of the leaf, do a U-turn, and come up through 3 beads on the other side. Repeat the process to create lobes on both sides of the central leaf form (figure 59).

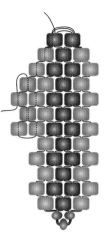

figure 57

figure 58

figure 59

Sea Form Embellishments

Flora and fauna of the sea can serve as excellent inspiration for a wide range of embellishments. Although some of these are the same as, or similar to, some floral embellishments—color and bead type can be altered to make a floral form look more aquatic—others are decidedly oceanic.

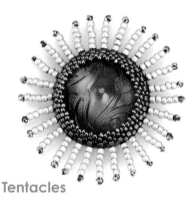

Tentacles

By changing the number of beads, bead color, and/or type of bead used, simple fringe can be transformed into oceanic forms. Tentacles can be made of any kind of bead, and there are infinite possibilities just within this simple form. By varying the length, you can capture the essence of a great variety of forms, from tiny bumps of coral, to the arms of anemones, to the long strands of kelp and other seaweeds.

The basic form is created by coming out of a bead or textile surface and threading up any number of beads (say, seven 11° seed beads). Do a U-turn and pass back through the first 6 beads, using the seventh as a stop bead (figure 60). As mentioned, variations on this form are infinite; I have illustrated a couple of options here.

The first variation uses a picot of 15°s at the end of the six 11°s, creating a more pointed tip (figure 61). It's a great way to

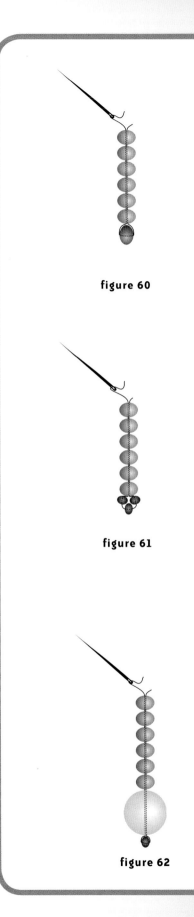

figure 60

figure 61

introduce a second size and color of bead into the basic tentacle. The second variation illustrates the possibilities that open up when you incorporate beads other than seed beads. This particular example shows 11° seed beads, a small freshwater pearl, and one 15° seed bead. By passing back through the pearl (using the 15° as the stop bead), you can create a tentacle with a bulbous end to it (figure 62). Changing the color of the beads creates an enormous variety of interesting oceanic tentacle forms.

Coral/Branch Fringe

Coral forms immediately bring to mind ocean life, and these are easily produced using seed beads and/or any variety of other types of beads. Although simple in concept, coral fringing can get quite elaborate and voluminous. It's an excellent way to fill out woven work, creating a lush and organic piece.

Basic coral fringe is made by stringing up any number of seed beads (for example, ten 11°s) that constitute the central stalk of the coral. Using the last bead as a stop bead, pass back through a couple of the previous beads—for example, the ninth and eighth beads (figure 63). String up more seed beads (say, three 11°s), use the last of these as a stop bead, and go back through the previous beads and into the central stalk (figure 63).

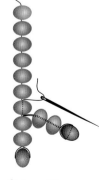

figure 62

figure 63

Pass through a couple beads in the central stalk (for example, the seventh, sixth, and fifth beads), and branch off again, stringing up more beads (for example, three 11°s). Use the last of these as the stop bead and go back through the previous beads and back into the central stalk (figure 64).

Pass through a couple more beads in the central stalk (for example, the fourth, third, and second beads). Branch off again, as previously described. The number and lengths of branches is entirely adjustable, as is the spacing between branches. Once you get to the top of the center stalk, pass through the first bead in the stalk and back into the beadwork or textile surface (figure 65).

There are infinite variations on this coral/branch fringe; just a couple are illustrated here. The first variation uses 15°s for the main stalk and branches of the coral, with one 11° bead as the stop bead on each branch (figure 66). A second variation uses 15°s for the main stalk and branches, with one 11°, a freshwater pearl, and a picot of 15° Czech charlottes at the tip of each branch. This adds a considerable amount of texture as well as the possibility for color variation within the coral form (figure 67). The final variation shows what I call multi-branching. Rather than making just single branches off of the central stalk, each of the branches has a number of offshoots, creating much lusher fringing (figure 68).

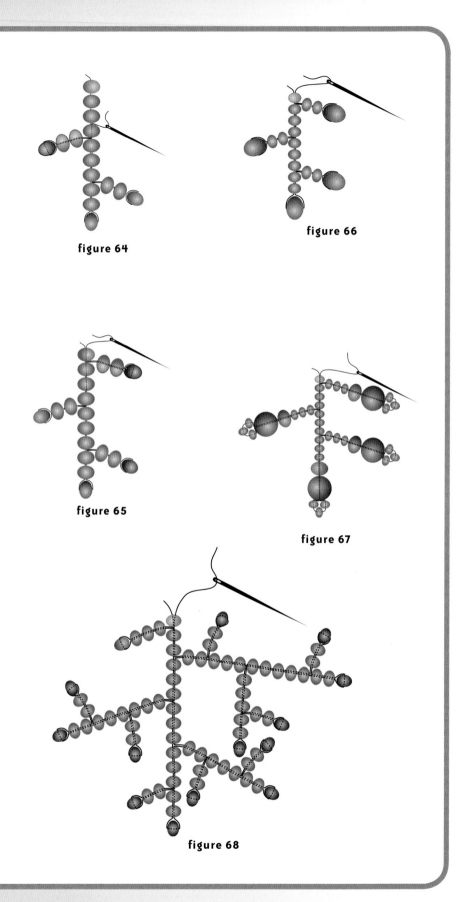

figure 64

figure 66

figure 65

figure 67

figure 68

Bubble Fringe

By changing the size, color, and/or types of beads, you can modify the berry cluster embellishment (page 30) to create aquatic bubble fringe. Use clear, pale blue, or AB-finish drops when making fringe to mimic water bubbles (figure 69).

Dagger Fringe

Dagger fringe is a variation of Bubble Fringe (this page). It's great for all sorts of oceanic forms and closely resembles the exquisite form of nudibranches (see page 53 for a photo of these lovely creatures). To create this variation of coral fringe, thread up size 11°s—3, for example—followed by four 15°s, a 5 x 16-mm Czech dagger, and 4 more 15°s. Go back through the last 11° (figure 70). Pick up 4 more 15°s, a dagger, and four 15°s. Go up through the next 11° (figure 71). Continue in this manner until you've come back up through the first of the 11°s. Stitch back into the bead-work or textile surface (figure 72).

Peyote Frond

Peyote frond is the same as frond form (page 32). By varying the color selection of the beads, bead sizes, and number of beads, you can effectively mimic the forms of sea fans and corals, as well as kelp or seaweed (figure 73).

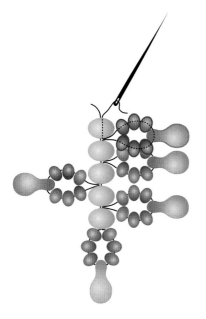

figure 69

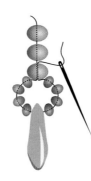

figure 70

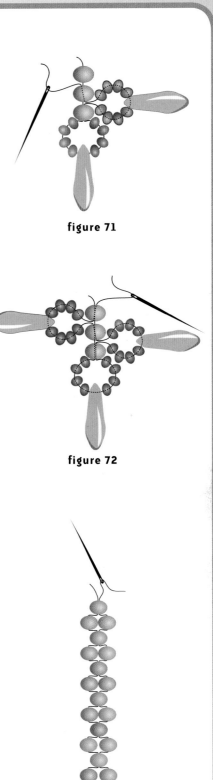

figure 71

figure 72

figure 73

Architectural Embellishments

A broad range of architectural forms could fall under the category of advanced embellishment structures. As with other embellishments, the possibilities are endless. Described here are a number of shapes I've worked with for you to consider and expound upon.

Rings and Rods

These forms are very geometric in nature and work well as structural embellishment elements in beadwork. Not only are they useful in creating toggle closures and beaded beads, but they can also be used as embellishments, as seen in the Ring and Toggle Bracelet (page 72). For more details on construction, see pages 23 and 24.

Pagoda

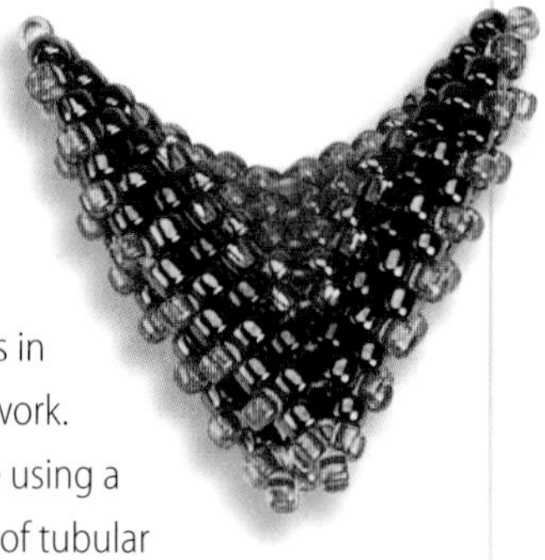

Time spent in Japan has inspired me to reproduce pagoda forms in woven beadwork. They're made using a combination of tubular Ndebele and increasing peyote stitch, creating solid, flared structures. These forms can be built independently and attached as individual elements to a larger piece, or worked directly off of a two-ladder Ndebele tube.

Using a wingspan of single thread, pick up four 15°s and tie a square knot to form a circle of beads. Leave about 10 inches (25.4 cm) of tail. Pass through 1 bead to hide the knot and then do 1 round, adding two 15°s between each 15° in the initial circle to create 4 ladders of Ndebele (figure 74). Working off of these 4 ladders, do another round of Ndebele, adding 2 beads to each ladder and 1 bead between each of the 4 ladders (figure 75).

After this point, continue doing Ndebele on each ladder and use peyote stitch between each ladder (figure 76). With each row, the peyote stitch will increase by 1 bead between each ladder, creating the flared appearance (figure 77). Once you've completed 5 rows in this manner, you're ready to do the final row. You'll notice that the form warps as it grows, with the Ndebele ladders creating up points and down points. On the final row, add one 15° on top of each of the 2 side Ndebele ladders, peyote stitch as usual in between, and then add a picot of three 15°s on each of the down Ndebele ladders (front and back side of the form).

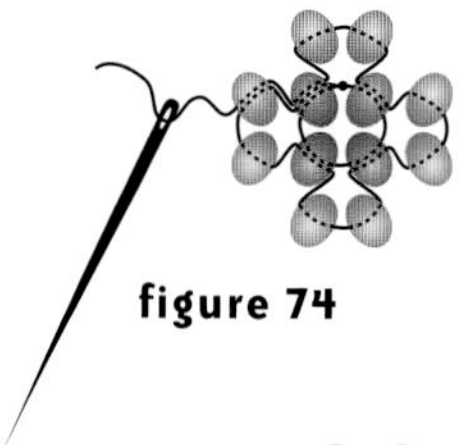

figure 74

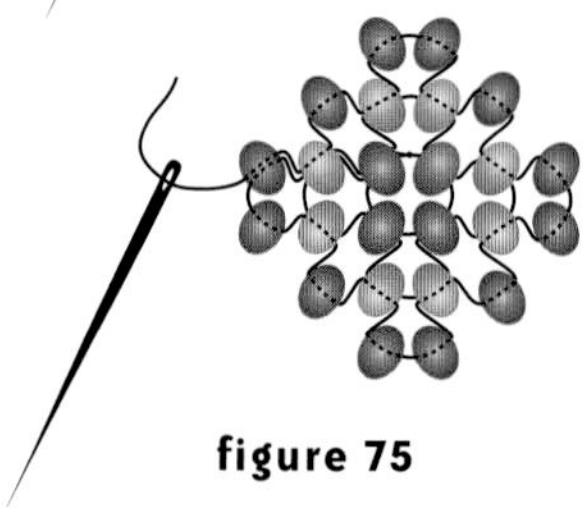

figure 75

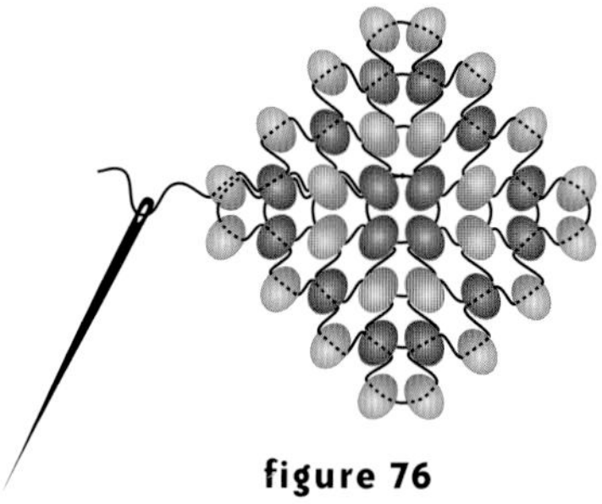

figure 76

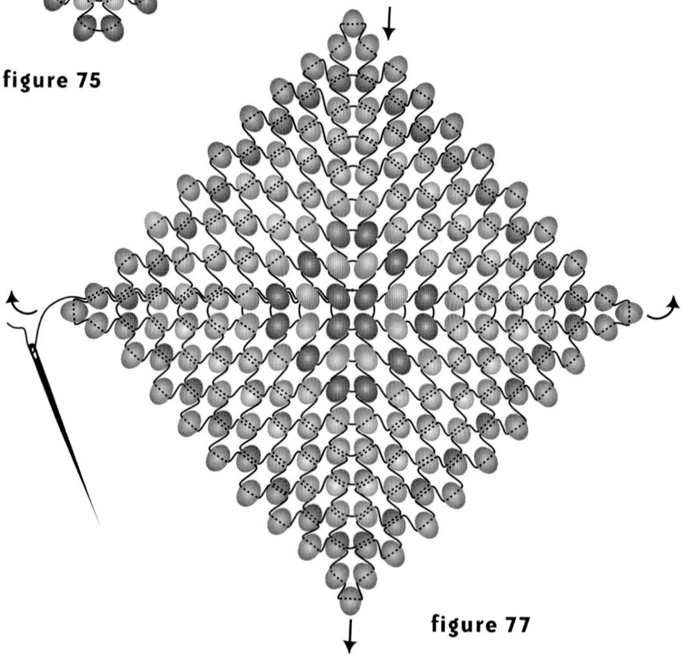

figure 77

Bell Flower

Although they're inspired by floral forms, these beaded flowers are distinctly more geometric than the floral embellishments earlier in the chapter. For that reason, I include them in this section.

Using a wingspan of single thread, pick up four 15° seed beads. Tie a square knot to form a circle of beads, leaving approximately 10 inches (25.4 cm) of tail. Go through 1 bead to hide the knot (figure 78). Do 1 round, adding two 15°s between each of the 4 beads to create 4 ladders of Ndebele. Step up at the end of this round (figure 79). Do another round of 15°s, this time adding 2 beads on each ladder and 1 bead in between each ladder. Step up at the end of the round (figure 80).

Do 1 round of Ndebele in 15°s, doing a 2-bead stitch on each of the 4 ladders of Ndebele, and adding 2 beads between each ladder (figure 81). Step up and do another round of Ndebele, this time adding 2 beads atop each of the 4 original ladders and also atop each of the 4 newly formed ladders between each of the original ladders (figure 82).

Weave 9 more rows of 8-ladder tubular Ndebele. Do a final row, adding one 15° on each ladder and one 3-mm magatama between each ladder, to create the flared effect at the base of the bell (figure 83).

As with the pagoda form, bell flowers can be made as separate elements and then attached to a larger piece of beadwork, or they can be worked directly off of tubular Ndebele.

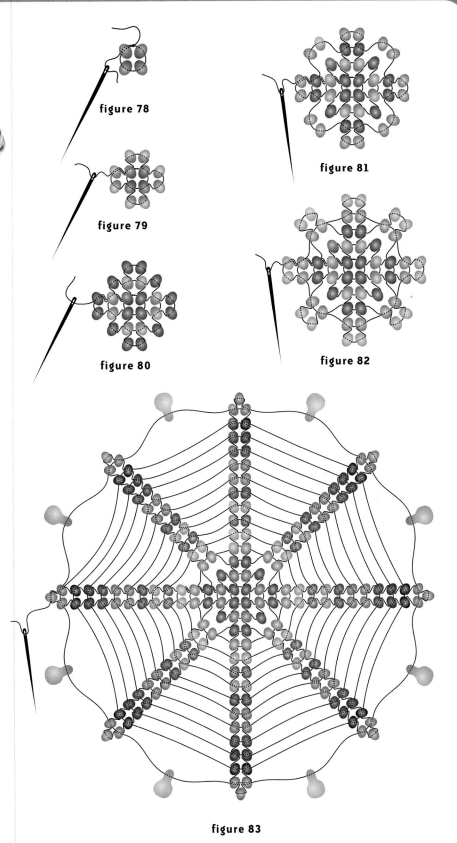

figure 78

figure 79

figure 80

figure 81

figure 82

figure 83

CHAPTER FIVE

APPROACHING COLOR AND DESIGN

When it comes to design inspiration, the planet is my muse. There's no greater source of inspiration than the natural world and the creatures and forms it encompasses.

Collecting Inspiration

Collecting inspirational forms and images is as much a part of the creative process as physically making something. Life frequently doesn't allow the time or the freedom for the immediate gratification of hands-on assembly. Some concepts need time to properly develop and mature. For these reasons, collecting is very important.

Inspiration comes in endless shapes and forms and from all aspects of life. It can arrive in the form of organic objects, such as flowers or leaves, or exist in more abstract forms like emotions or intuitions. Putting together an accessible collection of inspiration is essential to people involved in creative endeavors. For the forms and works contained in this book, most of my inspiration has been taken from flora and fauna forms. The final section of chapter 4 does address more architectural forms, but even these had organic origins.

The forms found in both the Eye Flower Pendant Necklace (page 94) and the Dahlia Necklace (page 119) were inspired by the dahlias I grow in my garden. © iStockphoto.com

There are many ways to go about collecting. I have a multitude of inspirational collections going at the same time. A great place to start is simply by gathering forms you find in nature and everyday life. When I take walks near my house, I frequently encounter inspiring flowers, leaves, and berries. At times I bring the actual items home with me for further inspection. If I need a more permanent record of a perishable item, I take photographs for my ideas file. Many of the projects in this book are derived from basic floral forms seen and collected near my home. The Lilac Earrings (page 59) are inspired by the lilac bushes in my front yard. The Indian Summer Sumac Necklace (page 105) finds its origins in the wild sumac berries across the street.

The endless images of artwork and historical costumes and artifacts (both in books and in art galleries and museums) are another valuable source of inspiration for me. These images are also important to my ideas file. In addition to collecting full shots of these pieces, I also like to crop out detail shots, which focus in on the texture, structure, and more intricate features. Often these details lead to development of designs and ideas that, while inspired by a larger piece, head down a path of their own. The Cherry Blossom Pendant Necklace (page 86) takes its inspiration from some of the turn-of-the-century colors and forms found in Art Nouveau period wallpaper, lithographs, and iconography.

A third source of inspiration for me is travel. My teaching takes me to new places around the world, and these experiences are invigorating and an incredible source of design ideas. I collect both objects and images from my travels, as well as make every

Laura McCabe

Blue Beauty, 2005

**Length, 68.6 cm;
centerpiece, 6.4 x 7.6 cm**

Antique prosthetic glass eyes, glass doll's eyes, glass seed beads, antique steel-cut beads, freshwater pearls, rose montées, Czech glass, leather; embroidery, peyote stitch, spiral rope, loop fringe, embellishment

Photo by Melinda Holden

attempt to learn about and understand the cultural differences that exist between these places and home. My travel collection has begun to manifest as a cabinet of curiosities. It is filled with many natural objects, handcrafts, and cultural oddities.

The *Blue Beauty* necklace is a perfect example of how such inspirational objects—in this case, antique prosthetic glass eyes purchased from an antique dealer—have become incorporated into a piece of wearable art.

Wild sumac grows in great abundance around my home. These are the dried berries, picked at the end of the fall after the plant has dropped its leaves. I find their forms so beautiful that I was inspired to make the Indian Summer Sumac Necklace (page 105).

This circa 1890 beaded cape is an exquisite example of Victorian bead embroidery at its finest. Beaded on silk and then fringed with delicate true-cut seed beads and 4-mm faceted fire-polished beads, this piece was most likely made in England or in the United States, although the beads came from the area we think of as the Czech Republic.

Working with Color

Color is a powerful inspirational source. The most spectacular and successful combinations of color often come courtesy of Mother Nature herself. The animals and plants we find in the natural world present fantastic and often unexpected color combinations. Look to these forms, collect them, photograph them, sketch them, and use them as starting points for developing successful palettes. I often advise students uncertain about color choices to collect any images that appeal to their color sense. Scraps of fabrics, photographs, and art or craft images that are appealing to your eye will work well as bead palettes. Fortunately, due to the vast number of bead colors available, it's almost always possible to match bead colors to any inspirational color combo you might have.

Coral polyps are the inspiration for the Anemone Ring on page 70. Ocean life, such as these exquisite forms, serves as excellent inspiration for beaded embellishment. Photo courtesy Florida Keys National Marine Sanctuary/NOAA

A uniquely bead-oriented issue is the tendency of beads to change or mutate in color once removed from their packaging and mixed with other bead colors. This is due to a number of factors, including the play of light that is more evident when beads are singled out from the whole. It can also be an effect of the increased intensity of color seen in a large grouping of same color beads, which then dissipates when these beads are viewed individually or in conjunction with beads of another color or finish. A great way to test-drive your beads is to pour a small amount of each of the colors you intend to use in your project into a pile. Mix these beads up and see how they look as a mixed group. Often, you can immediately see whether there's a color or colors that don't work within the palette as a whole. You may also consider gradual color transitions within the work rather than stark contrast in neighboring beads within the piece. This approach often mellows out overbearing, yet still desirable, bead colors.

The Pokeweed Berry Necklace (page 112) is an artistic interpretation of the pokeweed plants growing along the roadside near my house.
© iStockphoto.com

Realism vs. Artistic Interpretation

Woven beadwork has a whimsical and almost otherworldly look to it. The translucency and light play present in glass beads—along with their magical nature due to their captivating form and spiritual symbolism—lend a sense of fantasy to woven beadwork, in its multitude of forms. Although there can be a realistic interpretation of actual objects and images, I often prefer a more fantastical approach to beading, especially when creating heavily embellished organic forms.

Rather than work to accurately represent the form exactly as it may appear in nature or even in historical items of curious interest, I try to channel the feel or emotions conveyed by the object to create a fantasy-world version of the real-world piece. This reinterpretation may take the form of reassigning colors, using artistic license to reproduce a shape, or simply adding sparkling materials to elevate an ordinary object to a mystical level.

This photo of a nudibranch (left), which served to inspire the Nudibranch Bracelet above, came from one of my many stashed *National Geographic* magazines, filled with beautiful and inspiring photographs and articles. Photo by David Doubilet/National Geographic Stock

CHAPTER SIX
THE PROJECTS

GRAPE LEAF EARRINGS

A bold design incorporates both ring forms and peyote-stitched grape leaves to create a beautiful and wearable pair of earrings.

SUPPLIES

Basic Beading Kit (page 12)

Size 11° Japanese cylinder beads:

> Matte metallic sterling silver, 2 g
>
> Metallic dark purple, 1 g
>
> Chartreuse 24-karat gold lined, 3 g

Size 11° Japanese seed beads:

> Metallic dark plum, 1 g
>
> Chartreuse 24-karat gold lined, 1 g

Size 15° Japanese seed beads:

> Matte metallic sterling silver, 1 g
>
> Metallic dark purple, 1 g
>
> Metallic dark plum, 1 g

2 freshwater potato pearls, 6–7 mm

Sterling silver, gold, or gold-filled French ear wires, 1 pair

Chain-nose pliers

▶ Rings

The beaded rings are created with the technique described on page 23, using matte metallic sterling silver 15° seed beads and 11° cylinder beads. At this point, make only the basic ring—don't add the embellishment beads, because they'll be added later. Make 2 rings (with a starting circle of thirty-six 15°s). As you complete each ring, weave in and tie off the tail thread; keep the working thread to assemble and complete the earring later.

▶ Grape Leaves

Make the grape leaves using the technique described on page 41. Make 2, using metallic dark purple cylinder beads for the center vein of the leaf, and chartreuse 24-karat-lined cylinder beads as the primary color of the leaf. Bead all 3 picots on the leaf with metallic dark plum 15°s. Weave in and tie off the tail and working threads to complete the grape leaves (figure 1).

figure 1

▶ Assembly

1 Begin by adding a pearl to a ring form: Weave your working thread so it's coming out of the middle row of 15°s along the inside of the ring. Pick up a pearl and 3 metallic dark purple 15°s, pass back through the pearl, and go through the next bead in the middle row as shown in the upper portion of figure 2.

2 Weave your thread to the middle row of cylinder beads along the outside of the ring. Begin to peyote stitch a row with chartreuse 24-karat-lined 11°s; when you get to the space directly in line with the space where the pearl was added, pick up 7 matte metallic sterling silver 15°s and go through the next bead. This creates a loop to which the ear wires will be attached.

3 When you get to the space along the bottom of the ring, directly across from where the loop of 15°s was added, add the grape leaf. This is done by coming out of the cylinder bead in the ring, picking up 1 chartreuse 24-karat-lined 11°, and going down into the first of the 2 cylinder beads at the base of the leaf. Make a U-turn and come up through the cylinder bead next to it, then go back through the 11° and into the next cylinder bead along the middle row on the outside of the beaded ring. Continue adding chartreuse 24-karat-lined 11°s along the middle row of cylinder beads until the ring is completely surrounded (this is shown in the bottom part of figure 2).

4 Weave the thread into the next row up of cylinder beads, toward the top side of the ring, and create texture by adding 1 metallic dark plum 11° between every bead in the row (figure 3).

5 Once that round is complete, weave the thread to the topmost row of cylinder beads (the row closest to the 15°s along the inside of the ring), and create yet more texture by adding 1 metallic dark purple 15° between every cylinder bead in this row (shown in figure 3).

6 Attach an ear wire to the loop of 15°s at the top of the earring: Pry open the loop on the ear wire with chain-nose pliers, slip the loop of beads onto the ear wire, then close the ear wire. Repeat steps 1–5 to make the matching earring.

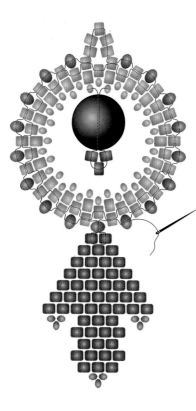

figure 2

figure 3

58

LILAC EARRINGS

The lilac bushes that bloom outside my front windows every spring inspired these elaborate earrings. The design illustrates the dimensional possibilities of flower cluster fringing when it's applied in bunches and when additional branches are added to the grouping. Although densely embellished, the earrings weigh relatively little.

▶ **Flower Clusters**

Refer to figure 1.

1 Thread up 2 wingspans (approximately 10 feet [3 m]) of thread. Wax well. Working with a single thread, thread 1 metallic dark plum 11° and circle back through it to create a stop bead. Leave 20 inches (50.8 cm) of tail.

2 String up metallic dark plum 11°s, with enough 11°s to create the desired length of the lilac earring. I usually string on 20, which creates a base stem about 1 inch (2.5 cm) long.

SUPPLIES

Basic Beading Kit (page 12)

Metallic dark plum 11°
Japanese seed beads, 5 g

Size 15° Japanese seed beads:
   Matte aqua pink lined, 5 g
   Chartreuse gold lined, 1 g
   Metallic dark purple, 1 g

3-mm Japanese magatamas:
   Amethyst green gold luster, 2 g
   Lavender silver lined, 2 g
   Blue-purple gold luster, 2 g

2 periwinkle freshwater pearls, 5.5 mm

6 Czech center-drilled glass leaf beads, 8 x 10 mm

Chartreuse gold-lined antique micro beads (optional; can be replaced with chartreuse gold-lined size 15°s), 2 g

French ear wires, 1 pair

Chain-nose pliers

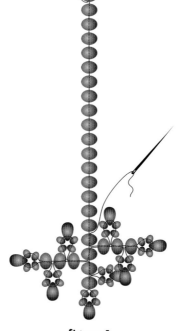

figure 1

3 Slide the 11°s down to the stop bead and begin flower cluster fringing. Pick up 2 matte aqua-pink-lined 15°s, 1 magatama, and 2 more 15°s and go back up through the last 11° on the base stem. Pick up 2 matte aqua-pink-lined 15°s, 1 magatama, and 2 more 15°s and go back up through the next 11° on the base stem.

4 Pick up 3 more metallic dark plum 11°s to create a branch off the base stem, pick up 2 matte aqua-pink-lined 15°s, 1 magatama, and 2 more 15°s and go back through the last 11° on the branch; continue to embellish, using this two 15°–1 magatama–two 15° series, between each 11° on this branch. When you get back to the base stem of 11°s, go back up through the next 11°. Add 3 more 11°s to create the next branch off the base stem. Pick up 2 matte aqua-pink-lined 15°s, 1 magatama, and 2 more 15°s, and go back through the last 11° on the branch; continue to embellish with 15°s and magatamas between each 11° on this branch. After adding 1 of these 3 berry clusters between the next two 11°s on the stalk, begin the branched clusters. As you work your way up the main stalk, increase the length of the clusters and gradually add more branching off of each base branch.

5 Continue adding embellished branches off the base stem in the manner described to create a thick cluster of magatama drops. (I add them without a defined color pattern, picking them up at random from the mix.) Gradually increase the length of the branches as you work your way up the base stem toward the stop bead to create the flower cluster effect. I usually use about ten 11°s in the last branch I add.

6 When you're 3 beads away from the stop bead, stop adding flower clusters—these last 4 beads, including the stop bead, are where the pearl, leaves, and loop will be added. Leave the working thread attached; you'll return to it later to add the leaf embellishments.

▶ Add the Pearl and Loop

1 Unthread the tail from the stop bead. Leave the stop bead on the thread. There should be four 11°s at this end of the flower clusters that have no embellishment between them.

2 Thread up the tail with a new needle and pick up 1 pearl and 9 metallic dark purple 15°s. Go back through the pearl to make a loop of beads and weave the tail off within the flower clusters, half hitching a couple times.

▶ Embellish with Leaves and Tendrils

As you work, refer to figure 2.

1 Return to the working thread used to create the flower cluster. Coming out of the 11° directly above the topmost flower cluster embellishments, pick up one 11°, 1 center-drilled leaf, and 3 chartreuse gold-lined 15°s. Go back through the leaf and the 11° and into the next 11° on the base stem, stitching toward the pearl.

2 Repeat this twice more, adding a total of 3 leaves.

3 Thread up a strand of micro beads or chartreuse gold-lined 15°s 1 to 2 inches (2.5 to 5.1 cm) long and wrap the strand around the stem at the base of the leaves in a spiral fashion to create a tendril form. The strand isn't tacked down, but simply wrapped around the base stem. When the wrapped strand reaches the pearl, weave the thread down through the 11°s. Weave off the tail thread within the flower clusters, half hitching 2 or 3 times before cutting the tail.

▶ Assembly

1 Attach an ear wire to the loop of 15°s at the top of the earring by prying open the loop on the ear wire with chain-nose pliers, then slipping the loop of beads onto the ear wire. Close the ear wire.

2 Repeat the process to make a second earring. You don't have to make them both identical; asymmetry adds to the organic feel of the form.

figure 2

HERRINGBONE CLUSTER EARRINGS

These beautiful cluster earrings are made using tubular herringbone that's embellished during the weaving process. Work the earrings from top to bottom, punctuating them with a delicate freshwater pearl.

SUPPLIES

Basic Beading Kit (page 12)

Size 11° Japanese seed beads:

   Metallic olive gold, 1 g

   Aqua 24-karat gold lined, 2 g

   Chartreuse 24-karat gold lined, 2 g

Teal 24-karat-lined size 15° Japanese seed beads, 1 g

24-karat-gold size 15° Czech charlotte beads, 2 g

32 jet AB2X (blue tone) crystal bicones, 3 mm

32 jet AB2X (green tone) crystal bicones, 4 mm

16 gold-colored freshwater pearls, 5.5 mm

2 blue freshwater pearls, 6 mm

French ear wires, 1 pair

Chain-nose pliers

61

Note: Japanese charlottes are *much* larger than Czech charlottes; the two are not interchangeable. Be sure to use the type described in the materials list.

▶ Bead Cluster

1 Cut 6 feet (1.8 m) of thread. Thread it onto a size 13 beading needle, and wax it well.

2 String up sixteen 15° seed beads. Leaving approximately 15 inches (38.1 cm) of tail, pass through the first bead again to create a circle of beads. Begin tubular her-ringbone: Pick up two 15° seed beads and go through the very next bead. Skip over 2 beads (thread on the outside) and go through the bead after that. Repeat 3 more times. With the last pass through, make sure the needle goes through the 15° that the tail thread is exiting. Step up through the next bead and pull in to create the 4-ladder herringbone start. For detailed directions on tubular herringbone, see page 21.

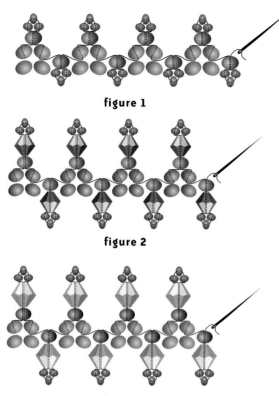

figure 1

figure 2

figure 3

3 Bead 1 round of herringbone with 11° seed beads in metallic olive gold. Bead the next round of herringbone with 11° seed beads in aqua 24-karat lined. From this point on, always use aqua 24-karat-lined 11°s for the core of the herringbone.

4 You're ready to add a round of simple picot embellishments. Make them by coming out of the first bead in the first ladder of herringbone and picking up 1 chartreuse 24-karat-lined 11° and three 15° charlottes. From this point on, always use a chartreuse 24-karat-lined 11° as the base bead in all embellishments. Go back through the 11° to form a picot of the charlottes, and down into the second bead in the first ladder of herringbone. Duplicate the embellishment sequence

between the first and second ladders, then come up through the first bead in the second ladder and repeat the embellishment a third time. Continue embellishing around the herringbone core. Upon its completion, you'll have 1 embellishment on top of, and 1 embellishment between, each ladder, for a total of 8 embellishments on that single round (figure 1).

5 Bead 1 round of normal herringbone with 11° seed beads.

6 Bead 1 round of 3-mm bicone embellishments. Do this by coming out of the first bead in the first ladder of herringbone and picking up 1 chartreuse 24-karat-lined 11°, one 3-mm crystal bicone, and three 15° charlottes. Go back through the bicone and the 11° to form a picot of charlottes.

Go back down into the second bead in the first ladder of herringbone. Repeat the embellishment sequence between the first and second ladders, then come up through the first bead in the second ladder and repeat the embellishment a third time. Continue in this manner, adding 1 embellishment on top of each ladder and 1 embellishment between each ladder, for a total of 8 embellishments in the round (figure 2).

7 Bead 1 round of normal herringbone with 11° seed beads.

8 Bead 1 round of 4-mm bicone embellishments by coming out of the first bead in the first ladder of herringbone and picking up 1 chartreuse 24-karat-lined 11°, one 4-mm crystal bicone, and three 15° charlottes. Go back through the bicone and the 11° to form a picot of charlottes. Go back down into the second bead in the first ladder of herringbone. Repeat the embellishment sequence between the first and second ladders, then come up through the first bead in the second ladder and bead an identical third embellishment. Continue in this way, adding 1 embellishment on top of each ladder and 1 embellishment between each ladder for a total of 8 embellishments in this round (figure 3).

9 Bead 2 rounds of normal herringbone with 11° seed beads.

10 Bead 1 round of pearl embellishments: Come out of the first bead in the first ladder of herringbone and pick up 1 chartreuse 24-karat-lined 11°, 1 gold-colored pearl, and three 15° charlottes. Go back through the pearl and the 11° to form a picot of the charlottes. Go back down into the second bead in the first ladder of herringbone. Repeat the embellishment sequence between the first and second ladders, then come up through the first bead in the second ladder and bead the embellishment a third time. Continue in this manner, adding 1 embellishment on top of each ladder and 1 between each ladder for a total of 8 embellishments in this round (figure 4).

11 Bead 2 rounds of normal herringbone with 11° seed beads.

12 Bead another round of 4-mm bicone embellishments (see step 8 above).

13 Bead 1 round of normal herringbone with 11° seed beads.

14 Bead 1 round of 3-mm bicone embellishments (see step 6 above).

15 Bead 1 round of normal herringbone with 11° seed beads.

▶ Add the Pearl

1 Add only 1 metallic olive gold 11° on top of each ladder of herringbone (figure 5).

2 Step up so the thread's coming out of the first of the 4 beads just added. Pick up a 6-mm blue pearl and three 15° charlottes. Go back through the pearl to create a picot of charlottes and into the 11° directly across from the bead just exited to create the embellishment (figure 6).

3 Make a second pass up through the pearl, through the picot, back through the pearl, and back into the bead the thread originally came out of.

4 Add 1 metallic olive gold 11° between each of the four 11°s added prior to making the pearl embellishment. Pull tight and weave in the tail, half hitching 2 or 3 times before cutting it off.

▶ Add the Loop

1 Using the tail thread at the top of the cluster, weave 1 row of regular herringbone using metallic olive gold 11°s.

2 Weave another row, this time adding only 1 metallic olive gold 11° on top of each ladder of herringbone.

3 Step up so you're coming out of the first of the 4 beads just added. Pick up nine 15° charlottes. Go through the 11° directly opposite the one you just exited from (figure 7).

4 Add 3 more 15° charlottes. Go through the middle 3 (of the 9) charlottes previously added, and then add 3 more 15° charlottes.

5 Go back into the original 11° you came out of to create the loop of charlottes, and weave in the tail, half hitching 2 or 3 times before cutting it off.

▶ Assembly

1 To attach an ear wire to the loop of 15° charlottes at the top of the earrings, pry open the loop on the ear wire with chain-nose pliers, slip the loop of beads onto the ear wire, then close the ear wire.

2 Repeat to make a second earring.

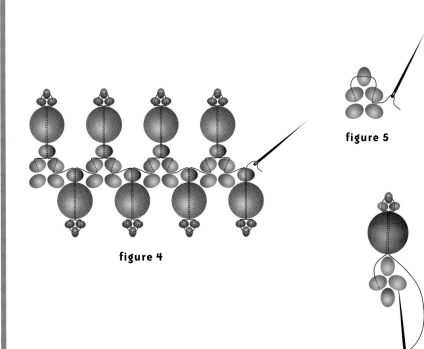

figure 4

figure 5

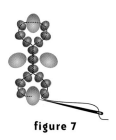

figure 6

figure 7

SUPPLIES

Basic Beading Kit (page 12)

Pale purple rose metallic gold hex-cut 11° Japanese cylinder beads, 5 g

Size 11° Japanese seed beads:
    Jonquil dichroic lined, 3 g
    Amethyst green gold luster, 3 g

Sterling silver size 15° Czech charlottes, 3 g

Size 15° Japanese seed beads:
    Jonquil dichroic lined, 2 g
    Opaline gilt lined, 2 g
    Opaline copper lined, 2 g
    Amethyst rainbow, 2 g
    Amethyst green gold luster, 2 g
    Gray-blue dichroic lined, 2 g

3 pale blue-purple freshwater pearls, 5 to 6 mm

6 Czech clear gold-lined glass rondelles, 2 x 4 mm

3 light Colorado topaz 2XAB crystal bicones, 3 mm

Matte metallic medium-blue 3-mm magatamas, 3 g

3 AB rose crystal montées, size 12ss

ROSEBUD RING

This beautiful ring incorporates several embellishment techniques, including Victorian-inspired rosebud forms, into a dimensional and organic ring. It's a beautiful match to the Rosebud Bracelet on page 67.

Note: Japanese charlottes are *much* larger than Czech charlottes; the two are not interchangeable. Be sure to use the type described in the materials list.

▶ Ring Band

1 The ring band serves as the base for the embellishments. It's woven in flat, even-count peyote (page 17) using Japanese cylinder beads. Make it 6 beads wide by the length of the desired band size.

2 Once the band is the desired length, embellish each side with 15° charlotte picots. Save this thread for later to zip up the band (figure 1).

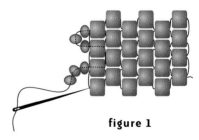

figure 1

► Rosebuds

1 Make 3 beaded rosebuds (page 36). For the project shown here, I used these:

Base Beads: Jonquil dichroic-lined 15's

Petal Row 1: Sterling silver 15° charlottes

Petal Row 2: Opaline gilt-lined 15's

Petal Row 3: Opaline copper-lined 15's

Petal Row 4: Amethyst rainbow 15's

Petal Row 5: Amethyst green gold luster 15's

Petal Row 6: Gray-blue dichroic-lined 15's

Petal Row 7: Gray-blue dichroic-lined 15's

► Embellish the Band

1 Embellish the ring band while it's still flat; it's so much easier than doing it in the round. (I generally use a doubled thread when embellishing a piece of beadwork that will be subjected to a lot of wear and tear.) Adding embellishments all the way around the band would make the ring uncomfortable to wear, so apply them only to the top side of the ring, in the central third of the band.

Work in a free-form manner using the following techniques:

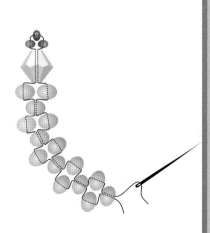

• **Simple Bud** (page 27) using 11° seed beads, pearls, rondelles, and charlottes (figure 2)

• **Frond Form** (page 32) using 11° seed beads, crystal bicones, and charlottes (figure 3)

• **Berry Cluster** (page 30) using 11° seed beads, 15° seed beads, and 3-mm magatamas (figure 4)

• **Lacy Stitch Rosebud** (page 36) attached with 11° seed beads, rondelles, and 15° seed beads (figure 5)

2 The rosebuds are attached as follows: Add the first rosebud near the center of the band strip. Weave in and secure the new thread and come out of a bead in the band. Depending on the desired stem length for the rose, pick up 1 to three 11° seed beads and one 2 x 4-mm rondelle. Go through the hole at the center of the

underside of the rosebud and pass the thread out through one of the outer holes on the back side. Pick up 1 rondelle and three 15° Japanese seed beads. Go back through the rondelle to make a picot of the 15°s, and go back through the outer hole and center hole on the back side of the bud, then down through the rondelle and the 11°s that constitute the stem and into the next bead in the band. As you pull the thread, guide the picoted rondelle inside the rosebud form. Pull down on the thread so the rose is held tightly against the ring band (figure 5).

figure 2

figure 3

Laura McCabe

Hairy Eyeball Pendant, 2008

Pendant, 6.4 x 7.6 cm

Antique prosthetic glass eye, glass seed
beads, rabbit fur, leather; bead embroidery,
peyote stitch

PHOTO BY MELINDA HOLDEN

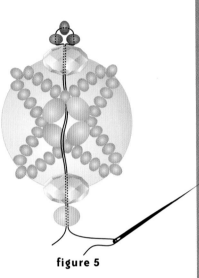

figure 5

3 Add another rosebud on each side of this
rosebud. These may be placed asymmetri-
cally on the band; to give the ring further
dimension, each rosebud can have a stem
of a different length. Next, add an assortment of simple bud, frond, and/or berry
cluster fringe forms to fill the center
third of the band and complete its
embellishment.

4 Zip the ends of the band together to create the tubular form of the ring. You may
have to add a picot to each side of the
band—where it was zipped together—to
complete the embellishment on the edges
of the band. Half hitch all threads 2 or 3
times before cutting the tails (figure 6).

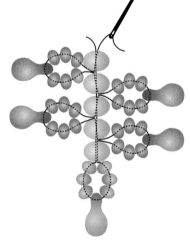

figure 4

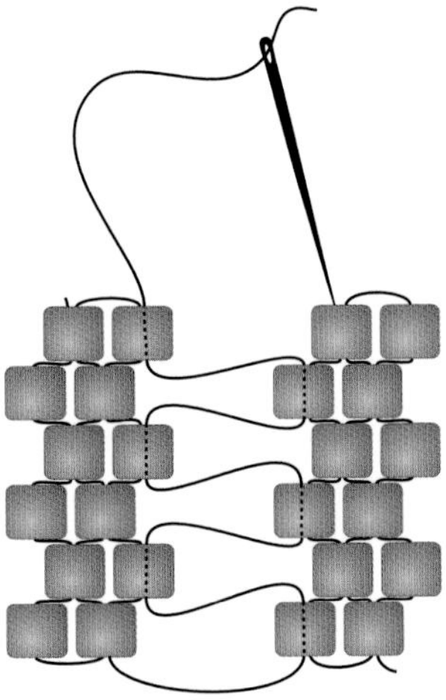

figure 6

ROSEBUD BRACELET

This lavishly decorated bracelet perfectly illustrates how combining multiple

embellishment forms can create elaborate textures within a small space.

Note: Japanese charlottes are *much* larger than Czech charlottes; the two are not interchangeable. Be sure to use the type described in the materials list.

▶ Bracelet Band

The bracelet band that serves as the base for the embellishments is woven in flat, even-count peyote using Japanese cylinder beads. (See page 17 for instruction on this stitch.) The weaving begins from the buttonhole end of the bracelet band.

1 Single thread approximately 5 feet (1.5 m) of beading thread on a size 12 beading needle. Wax well.

2 Pick up 8 cylinder beads. Slide them down the thread, leaving a tail about 12 inches (30 cm) long. Hold the beads on the thread to prevent them from sliding off the end. Change direction and pick up 1 cylinder bead and begin weaving flat, even-count peyote stitch.

3 Weave back and forth until you've completed 6 rows of peyote stitch (count 3 beads up each side).

4 Construct the buttonhole portion of the band: Begin the next row as usual, but after putting on the first bead, pick up another bead, change direction, and go through the bead you just added. Weave back and fourth in this manner to create a strip of flat peyote stitch 2 beads wide by 19 rows long (count 9 beads along the inside of the strip and 10 along the outside of the strip). Your working thread will be to the inside of the buttonhole (figure 1).

5 Thread the tail thread on a size 12 English beading needle. Weave the tail into the initial 6 rows of peyote and turn around to begin a strip of peyote stitch 2 beads wide (as in step 4). Weave back and forth until this 2-bead-wide strip is 19 rows long (count 10 beads along the inside of the strip and 9 along the outside of the strip). The thread will be to the outside of the bracelet.

6 Resume beading with the working thread from the original strip of beads. Pick up 4 cylinder beads, and go through the last 2 beads on the second strip of beads (shown in figure 1).

7 Resume flat, even-count peyote stitch. This connects the narrow strips and creates the buttonhole. Continue in this stitch until the bracelet is the desired length (see box at bottom right.)

8 Using a new thread, stitch the button on by coming out of the flat peyote, picking up one 11°, passing through 1 of the holes in the button (from the back to the front), picking up three 15°s and going back through the second hole in the button (from front to back). Pick up 1 more 11° before going into the peyote band.

(Using a new thread to attach the button helps ensure that if the button falls off in the future, the integrity of the bracelet won't be compromised.)

9 Complete the band by adding 15° Czech charlotte picots along the edge. To bead this edging, come out of one of the corner cylinder beads along the outer edge, pick up three 15° charlottes, and go into the next cylinder bead. Turn around within the beadwork and come out of the next cylinder bead. Pick up 3 more 15°s and go into the next cylinder bead (figure 2). Continue in this manner until the entire bracelet is edged with picots. At the ends of the bracelet band, peyote stitch just 1 charlotte between each of the up cylinder beads. The picots not only provide a nice finished look to the bracelet band, but they also cover up the thread that would otherwise show along the edge of the band.

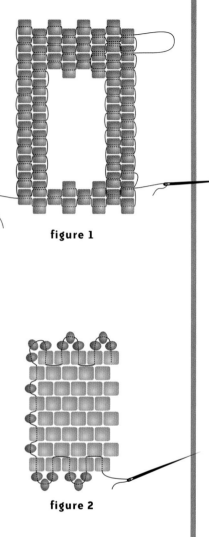

figure 1

figure 2

Determine the length of the bracelet by measuring from the far edge of the buttonhole to the location of the center of the button. You must bead the bracelet band about ¾ inch (1.9 cm) beyond the location of the center of the button.

▶ Rosebuds

1 Bead 10 to 20 Lacy Stitch Rosebuds (page 36), depending on the size of the base band and the quantity of flowers you desire. Make them using the same bead sizes and colors as listed for the Rosebud Ring on page 65.

▶ Embellish the Band

1 Add embellishments over the entire bracelet, except where the button and the buttonhole are so you can comfortably button and unbutton the bracelet. (Use a doubled thread because this piece of beadwork will be subjected to lots of wear and tear.)

Work in a free-form fashion using the following techniques:

- **Simple Bud** (page 27) using 5- to 6-mm pearls, rondelles, and 15° charlottes (figure 3)

- **Frond Form** (page 32) beaded with 11° seed beads, 3-mm crystal bicones, and 15° charlottes (figure 4)

- **Berry Cluster** (page 30) using 11° seed beads, 15° seed beads, and 3-mm magatamas (figure 5)

- **Branch Fringe** (page 43) using 11° seed beads, 3-mm crystal bicones, and 15° charlottes (figure 6)

- **Lacy Stitch Rosebuds** (page 36), attached using 11° seed beads, rondelles, and 15° seed beads

2 Add the rosebuds in a random manner, placing some in groups next to each other and leaving gaps between others. I then add other embellishments to fill the spaces between the rosebuds. Mixing forms adds to the dimensional interest of the bracelet.

Attach the rosebuds as follows: Weave in and secure the new thread and come out of a bead in the band. Depending on the desired stem length for the rose, pick up 1 to three 11° seed beads and a 2 x 4 mm rondelle. Go through the hole at the center of the underside of the rosebud and pass the thread out through one of the outer holes on the back side. Pick up 1 rondelle and three 15° seed beads. Go back through the rondelle to make a picot of the 15°s, go back through the outer hole and center hole on the back side of the bud, and down through the rondelle and the 11°s that constitute the stem and into the next bead in the band. As you pull the thread, guide the picoted rondelle inside the rosebud form. Pull down on the thread so the rose pulls tightly down against the bracelet band (figure 7).

3 Weave in any tail threads, half hitching once or twice before cutting the tails.

figure 3

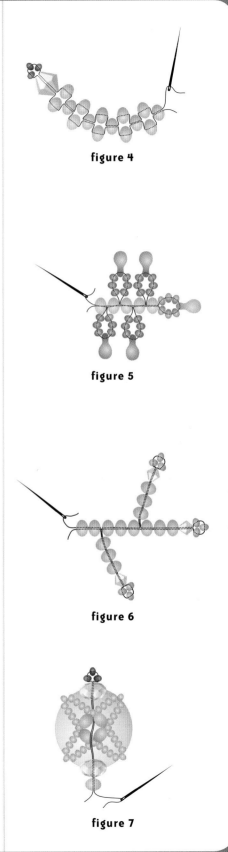

figure 4

figure 5

figure 6

figure 7

SUPPLIES

Basic Beading Kit (page 12)

Glass cabochon, size may vary*

Metallic 24-karat gold lavender rose gold size 11° Japanese cylinder beads, 5 g

Size 11° Japanese seed beads:

> **Matte topaz pink lined, < 1 g**

> **Matte blue-purple lined, < 1 g**

Size 15° Japanese seed beads:

> **Matte blue-purple lined, 2 g**

> **Semi-matte orchid gilt lined, 2 g**

> **Semi-matte salmon gilt lined, 2 g**

> **Semi-matte orange gilt lined, 2 g**

> **Matte metallic sterling silver, 2 g**

Matte metallic sterling silver size 15° Japanese charlotte beads, 2 g

***The one shown here is approximately 20 mm in diameter.**

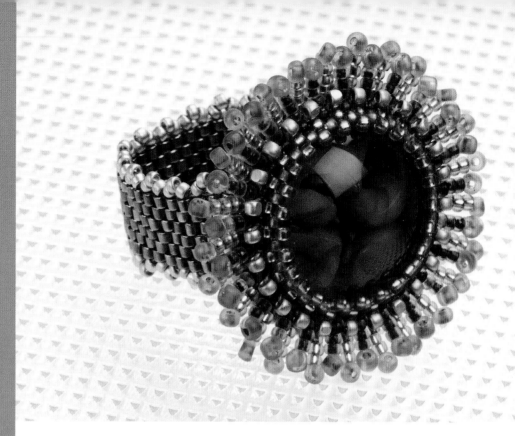

ANEMONE RING

This fabulous cocktail ring is made with a glass cabochon—I used a piece by Gregory Hanson of Portland, Oregon, but your favorite bead store may stock work by any number of terrific artists. With a tentacle embellishment (page 42), a simple bezeled cabochon is transformed into a captivating beaded anemone.

Note: Japanese charlottes are *much* larger than Czech charlottes; the two are not interchangeable. Be sure to use the type described in the materials list.

▶ Bezeled Cabochon

1 Cut 10 feet (3 m) of thread, thread it onto a size 12 beading needle, and wax it well.

2 Thread up enough cylinder beads to fit exactly around the widest part of the cabochon. This *must* be an even number of beads; if an odd number is the perfect fit, add 1 bead to make the count even.

3 Tie a knot in the circle of beads, leaving about 12 inches (30.5 cm) of tail. Don't pull the circle of beads together tightly; leave about 2 to 3 bead-widths of thread showing in the circle of beads. Begin peyote stitching with cylinder beads. Bead 2 rounds of peyote stitch.

4 Switch to size 15° seed beads. The number of rows to weave using the size 15° seed beads depends on the size of your cabochon. You'll work the back side of the bezel, so the determining factor is how many rows are required to keep the stone from falling through. The ring shown here has 3 rows of 15°s, which is probably about average. I usually change color with each row as a way of introducing more color into the design (figure 1).

5 After completing the back side, weave up to the topmost row of cylinder beads and place the cabochon, right side up, into the setting. Build the sides of the bezel with rows of cylinder beads. Follow this by adding rows of 15°s that cup in over the edge of the cabochon to hold it in place. The number of rows will vary depending on the size and thickness of the cab. You may need to do several rows of cylinder beads before reaching the point where the sides of the cabochon transition to the top of the cabochon. Switching to 15°s pulls the beadwork in, tightening it over the edge of the cabochon to secure it firmly in place. Bead as many rows of 15°s as required to hold the cabochon firmly.

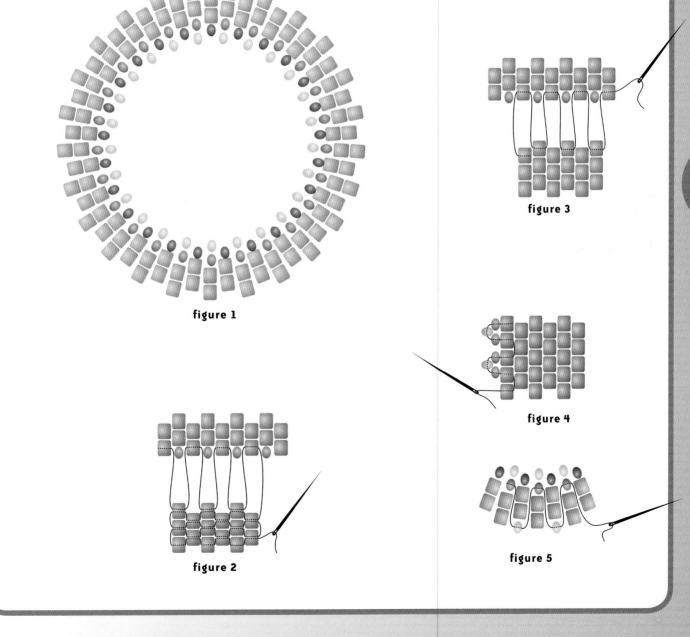

figure 1

figure 2

figure 3

figure 4

figure 5

▶ Ring Band

1 Weave your working thread down to the bottommost row of cylinder beads (toward the back side of the cabochon). Begin weaving a strip of flat, even-count peyote stitch directly off of this row, using cylinder beads. The width of this strip can vary. In the ring shown here, the band is 6 cylinder beads wide (figure 2). In terms of band width, the greatest determining factor is cabochon size. For smaller cabochons, I frequently do 4-bead-wide bands.

2 Weave the strip long enough so that when it's joined to the other side of the cabochon it extends comfortably around the finger, resulting in the desired ring size. Zip the last row of the strip into the bottom row of cylinder beads directly across from where you began the strip (figure 3).

3 Embellish the edges of the ring band with picots of 15° seed beads (figure 4).

▶ Embellish the Bezel and Add Tentacles

1 To begin the bezel embellishment, weave your thread up to the bottommost row of 15° seed beads on the top side of the bezel. Using peyote stitch, add one 15° Japanese charlotte between every 15° in this row. This adds a row of simple studs to the bezel surface (figure 5).

2 After adding the charlottes, step down 1 row and create a row of tentacles (page 42). Each tentacle is made using three 15°s and one 11° as the stop bead. Add the tentacles between each bead in this row (figure 6).

3 Step down 1 row and add a second row of tentacles, this time using four 15°s and one 11° as the stop bead (figure 7).

4 If the depth of the bezel allows, you can add 1 or 2 rows of 15° Japanese charlotte beads (described in step 1 of this section) to add more texture below the tentacles (figure 8).

5 Weave in any tail threads, half hitching a couple times before burying and cutting off the tail.

figure 6

figure 7

figure 8

Laura McCabe
Ring and Toggle Bracelet, 2009
3.8 x 19 cm

Glass seed beads, freshwater pearls; peyote stitch, embellishment

PHOTO BY STEWART O'SHIELDS

72

STONE CABOCHON BRACELET

Create this stylish bracelet by combining beaded bezel stone cabochons—

embellished with crystals and pearls—with beaded ring forms.

Note: Japanese charlottes are much larger than Czech charlottes; the two are not interchangeable. Be sure to use the type described in the materials list.

▶ Bezel the Stones

1 Glue each of the stone cabochons to separate pieces of leather. The pieces of leather should be about ½-inch (1.3 cm) larger than the cabochons on all sides. Using a toothpick, apply an even coat of adhesive to the backs of the cabochons. Place the sticky side of the cabochon down on the right side (the smooth side) of the leather, being sure to maintain a ½-inch (1.3 cm) border of leather around the perimeter of the stone. Allow the adhesive to dry for at least 10 minutes.

2 Beginning with the first cabochon, sew the bezel's foundation row of beads along the perimeter of the stone. Single thread approximately 6 feet (1.8 m) on a size 12 beading needle, and wax well. Tie a knot at the end and cut, leaving a ¼-inch (6 mm) tail. Pass the needle up through the leather from the back side, coming up next to the cabochon. Pull the thread tight so the knot is snug to the leather. String on 6 pink copper-lined cylinder beads, slide them down the thread to the edge of the cabochon, place them in a line closely against the stone, and then stitch down through the leather at the end of the line formed by the beads. Sew back up through the leather with the needle coming through the leather between beads 3 and 4, and then pass through beads 4, 5, and 6 again, creating an embroidery backstitch (figure 1).

3 Continue this 6-bead embroidery backstitch around the perimeter of the cabochon. As you finish this row, make sure the row contains an even number of beads;

you may need to adjust the number of beads in the final stitch to accomplish this. Travel through this row of beads one more time, to ensure good tension.

4 Begin peyote stitching upward from the base row: Pick up a bead, skip a bead, go through a bead (figure 2). Continue peyote stitching with cylinder beads for a couple rows, until you reach the curve in the cabochon (the number of rows will vary with the thickness of the cabochon). When the cabochon starts to curve in, switch to size 15's—the decrease in bead size will cause the bezel to curve inward, creating a tight fit. Stitch 2 rows of 15's. Pull each bead tightly into place. The cabochon should be securely held by the bezel; if it's not, you may need to add a row or two more of 15's. Finally, add a final row using gold 15° Czech charlottes. Again, pull each bead tightly into place. (**Note:** The row count for both cylinder beads and 15's will vary depending on the height of your cab.)

5 Weave the thread back through the beads to the base row and pass through the leather. Come back up through the leather next to the outside of the foundation row of the beaded bezel. Backstitch one more row using pink copper-lined cylinder beads (6 at a time, as before), placing the beads snugly alongside the foundation row. As you finish this row, make sure it contains an even number of beads; if necessary, adjust the number of beads in the final stitch to accomplish this. Pass through this row a couple of times to straighten up the row of beads. Weave through to the back side, knot off, and cut the thread.

6 Repeat the process described above for the remaining stone cabochons.

▶ Embellish the Bezels

1 Cut 10 feet (3 m) of thread (use FireLine, because the edges of the holes of the crystal beads are sharp), thread it through a needle, and double it. Tie a knot at the end and cut, leaving a ¼-inch (6 mm) tail. Pass the needle up through the leather from the back side, coming up between the bezel and the row of embroidery. Pull the thread tight so the knot is snug against the leather. Weave up to the top row of cylinder beads on the bezel.

2 Add 1 crystal bead between every bead on this row (figure 3). After completing the round, weave back down through the bezel and knot off the thread on the back side of the leather.

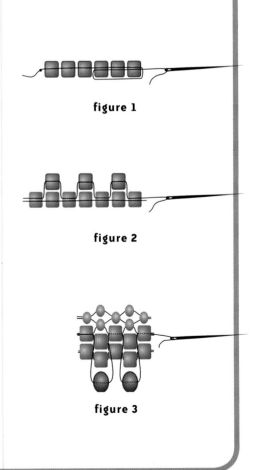

figure 1

figure 2

figure 3

▶ Attach the Leather Backing

1 Begin a new single thread with approximately 6 feet (1.8 m) of nylon thread in a color that matches your leather, and knot the end, as before. Pass the thread up through the leather, coming out between the bezel and the beads in the outer base row.

2 Using a toothpick, apply adhesive to the wrong side (the rough side) of the leather, taking care not to smear any on the thread hanging from the front side. Place the second piece of leather over the leather on the back side of the cabochon, right side (smooth side) out, and press to ensure evenness. Allow it to dry for at least 10 minutes.

3 Cut away any excess leather, leaving a small edge—about the width of a row of cylinder beads. Using the thread already attached to the piece, pass the needle through both pieces of leather to the back side and overhand stitch the entire perimeter of the piece. This ensures the backing won't come off and gives a nice finished look to the piece.

4 After completing the overhand stitching, pass the needle back up through both pieces of leather and through a couple of beads in the outer base row. Begin peyote stitching outward, to cover up the leather edge. Peyote stitch 1 row of cylinder beads. Leave the thread attached; you can use it later when connecting the bezeled stones together and adding the pearl embellishments.

5 Repeat the same backing technique for each of the other stone cabochons.

▶ Beaded Rings

1 The 2 beaded rings needed for this project are made using the basic ring technique described on page 23. Each ring begins with a circle of 36 size 15° seed beads.

2 When the first ring is completed, weave a tab of peyote stitch that's 4 beads wide off of the center row of cylinder beads on the ring. This tab should be 4 rows long (count 2 beads up each side).

3 After this first tab is made, weave over 14 beads and peyote stitch a second tab that's 4 beads wide by 7 rows long (count 3 beads up one side and 4 up the other). This ring will be attached to the toggle loop.

4 Add one 11° seed bead between each cylinder bead along the center row in the ring (except for where the tabs are).

5 Weave your thread down to the middle row of 15°s along the inside of the ring. Travel through the beads until you're coming out of the 15° that's midway between the 2 tabs added on the outside of the ring.

6 Pick up one 11°, 1 stone bead, and 1 more 11°. Go through the 15° directly opposite the one you came out of on the other side of the ring. Now pass back through the 11°, the stone bead, the 11°, and into the original 15° you came out of (figure 4).

7 Weave off the tail threads, half hitching a couple of times before cutting the ends.

8 The second ring is made in exactly the same manner—*except* you should make the second tab (the one that was 4 beads wide by 7 rows long on the previous ring) 2 beads wide by 20 rows long (count 10 beads up each side). This ring will be attached to the toggle bar. As with the previous ring, add the 11°, the stone bead, and the 11° across the inside of the ring at a 90° angle from where the tabs are placed (figure 5).

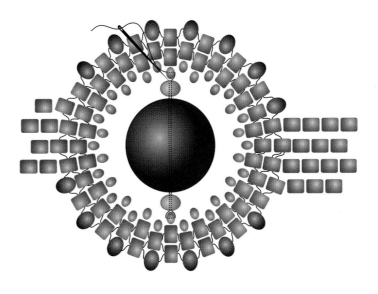

figure 4

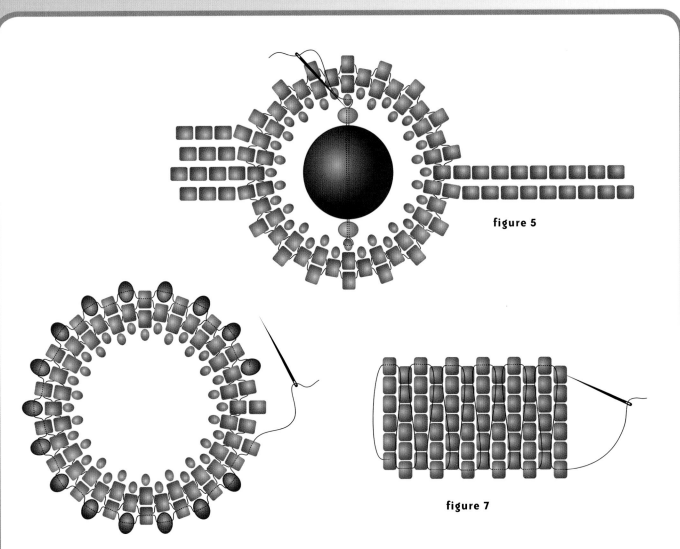

figure 5

figure 6

figure 7

▶ Toggle Ring

1 The toggle ring is made using the basic ring form described above, starting with a circle of 36 size 15° seed beads (figure 6).

2 When the ring in complete, zip it to the 4-bead-wide/7-row-long tab on the first of the rings described above.

3 Embellish the center row of cylinder beads on the toggle ring by adding one 11° between every bead in this row.

4 Embellish both sides of the connector tab with 15° Czech charlotte picots.

▶ Toggle Bar

1 Refer to figure 7 as you work. Weave a strip of even-count peyote 12 beads wide and 12 rows long (count 6 beads up each side).

2 Zip the strip to itself to make a bar, and embellish the ends with a round pearl. Select pearls that are about 5 mm in diameter. For detailed directions on making this toggle bar form, refer back to page 24 in chapter 3.

3 Zip the completed bar to the 2-bead-wide/20-row-long tab on the second of the rings described above.

4 Embellish both sides of the connector tab with 15° Czech charlotte picots.

► Assembly

The bracelet is linked using tabs of even-count peyote stitch that are woven off the outer row of cylinder beads around the bezeled stones.

1 Begin by working off of the outer row of peyote-stitched cylinder beads on the cabochon that will be at the center of the bracelet. Using the thread you left attached, weave a tab 6 beads wide by 6 or more rows long (this length can vary depending on what you want the finished length of the bracelet to be). See figure 8.

You can determine the length the connectors off of the center cabochon need to be by laying out the components next to each other—the toggle ring, the 3 bezeled cabochons, and the toggle bar—in the order they'll be assembled. Measure the length from the toggle bar to the far inside edge of the toggle ring. Compare to your desired length. Divide the difference between the desired length and the measured length by 2. This is the length each of the 2 tabs off of the central cabochon needs to be.

2 Zip the tab into the next stone and embellish both sides of the tab with picots of 15° charlottes (figure 9).

3 Work your thread around to the other side of the cabochon and weave a tab 6 beads wide by 6 or more rows long (this length can vary depending on what you want the finished length of the bracelet to be). Zip the tab into the next stone and embellish both sides of the tab with picots of 15° charlottes.

As a general rule, the tabs are placed opposite each other, although this isn't always true, particularly if you're using free-form cabochons.

4 After linking the stones, zip the toggle bar to a cabochon on one end and the toggle loop to the cabochon on the other end using the 4-bead-wide/4-row-long tab on each of the closure components. Zip the tabs into the outer row of cylinder beads on the stone bezels and embellish both sides of the tab with 15° charlottes.

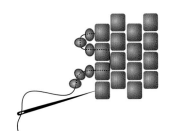

figure 8

figure 9

▶ Embellish the Edges

1 Using the attached thread, add 1 row of peyote stitch—using size 11° seed beads—to the outermost row of cylinder beads around the cabochons. The 11°s are added everywhere except where there are connector tabs (figure 10—the bezel beads are not shown).

2 After the 11°s have been added, you're ready to add the pearl embellishments. The pearl embellishments are added between every cylinder bead in the outermost row of cylinder beads (the row the 11°s were added to). To add them, pick up one 11°, 1 pearl (either a keshi [figure 11] or a round pearl [figure 12]), and a single 15° charlotte on top of the keshi pearls or a picot of three 15° Czech charlottes on top of the round pearls. Go back through the pearl and the 11° and into the next bead in the row of cylinder beads.

3 Add pearl embellishments between every bead in the outermost row of cylinder beads around each stone. Make the majority of them with keshi pearls, with round pearl embellishments randomly scattered throughout. After embellishing around 1 stone, weave over to the next cabochon and continue embellishing. After embellishing the cabochons, you may add a few pearl embellishments to the toggle ring and the toggle bar connector tabs. When embellishing the toggle connector tab, add only a few pearl embellishments near the beaded ring. (This will allow the toggle bar to easily slide into the toggle ring.)

If you have trouble keeping good tension on your embellishments while weaving with a single thread, change to double thread to increase the tension.

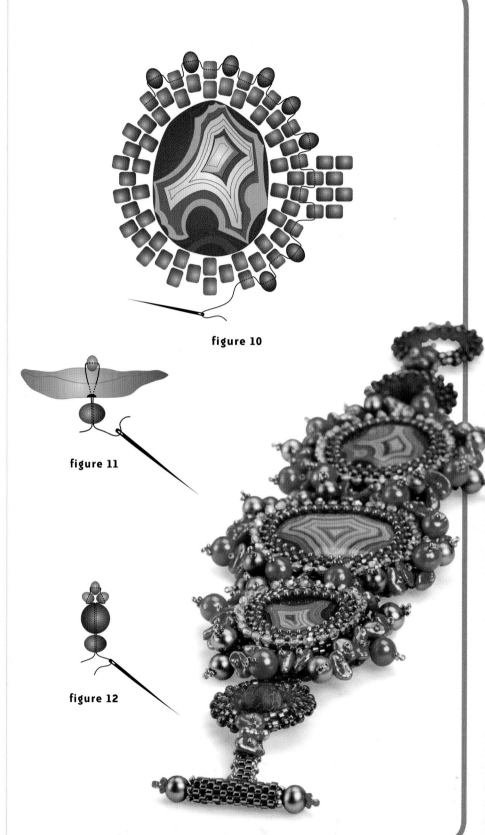

figure 10

figure 11

figure 12

TOP LEFT

Laura McCabe

Willow Creek Jasper Necklace, 2007

Length, 48.3 cm

Willow creek jasper stone points by
Gary Wilson, glass seed beads, freshwater pearls, crystal beads, Czech glass
beads, cubic zirconia beads; peyote
stitch, herringbone stitch, branch
fringe, embellishment

PHOTO BY MELINDA HOLDEN

TOP RIGHT

Laura McCabe

Space Shot, 2009

7.6 x 7.6 x 7.6 cm

Blue-gold stone points by Gary Wilson,
glass doll's eyes, feathers, glass seed
beads, crystal beads; peyote stitch,
embellishment

PHOTO BY MELINDA HOLDEN

BOTTOM

Laura McCabe

Mudcrack Necklace, 2008

Length, 49.5 cm

Fossilized mudcracks by Gary Wilson,
glass seed beads, freshwater pearls,
crystal beads, Czech glass, leather;
peyote stitch, herringbone stitch,
embellishment

PHOTO BY MELINDA HOLDEN

SUPPLIES

Basic Beading Kit (page 12)

Size 15° Japanese seed beads:

> **Teal 24-karat gold lined, 3 g**
>
> **Matte metallic blue-purple, 4 g**
>
> **Bright blue-purple semi-matte gilt lined, 2 g**

Marcasite or sterling silver 15° Czech charlotte beads, 1 g

8 matte metallic silver 15° Japanese charlottes

2 pale peacock blue freshwater pearls, 6 mm

2 periwinkle freshwater pearls, 5.5 mm

2 light sage-green freshwater pearls, 5.5 mm

16 aqua teal-lined magatamas, 3 mm

French ear wires, 1 pair

Chain-nose pliers

BELL FLOWER EARRINGS

These lovely earrings take their inspiration from bluebells, some of the first flowers to emerge every spring. Construct them by weaving a bell flower form on an Ndebele base and embellishing each end of the base with pearls.

Note: Japanese charlottes are *much* larger than Czech charlottes; the two are not interchangeable. Be sure to use the type described in the directions.

▶ Core

1 Cut 6 feet (1.8 m) of thread. Thread it onto a size 12 beading needle, and wax it well.

2 String up 8 teal 24-karat-lined 15° seed beads. Leaving a 10-inch (25.4 cm) tail, pass through the first bead to create a circle of beads. Don't tie a knot.

3 Pick up 2 teal 24-karat-lined 15°s and go through the very next bead in the circle of 8. Skip over 2 beads in the circle—with the thread on the outside of the beads—and go through the next bead. Repeat these steps again and step up through one bead. When you pull tightly on the tail and working thread, 3 rows of 2-ladder tubular Ndebele should emerge. For more information on tubular Ndebele, see page 21.

4 Weave a total of 14 rows of tubular Ndebele (including the initial 3 from the start).

▶ Add Pearls to the Bottom

1 Coming out of the first bead in the first ladder, pick up 1 pale peacock blue pearl, 1 periwinkle pearl, and three 15° Czech charlottes.

2 Go back up through both pearls and into the second bead in the first ladder of Ndebele.

3 Come back down through the first bead in the second ladder of Ndebele and pass through the pearls, the charlotte picot, back up through the pearls, and into the second bead in the second ladder of Ndebele.

4 Pass up through 13 of the 14 rows of core beads. Leave your working thread attached, coming out between these rows. You'll return to it later to weave the bell flower.

▶ Add a Pearl to the Top

1 Thread up the tail. If necessary, pass up through a bead so it's coming out of the first bead of a ladder in the top row of Ndebele.

2 Coming out of the first bead in the first ladder of Ndebele, pick up 1 light sage green pearl and eleven 15° Czech charlottes. Go back down through the pearl and into the second bead in the first ladder of Ndebele.

3 Come back up through the first bead in the second ladder of Ndebele, pass through the pearl, the charlottes, back through the pearl, and into the second bead in the second ladder of Ndebele.

4 Come back up through the first bead in the first ladder of Ndebele, pick up 1 matte metallic silver 15° Japanese charlotte, and go down through the second bead in this ladder. Add another 15° Japanese charlotte between the 2 ladders before passing up through the first bead in the second ladder. Repeat this process again, adding a total of 4 Japanese charlottes—2 on top of the ladders and 2 in between the ladders.

5 Add 1 teal 24-karat-lined 15° seed bead between each Japanese charlotte, for a total of four 15°s added. This creates a nice base around the sage green pearl. Weave off this thread, being sure to half hitch a couple times before burying the thread.

▶ Bell Flower

1 Return to the working thread that you left off with previously; it should be coming out between the topmost row of Ndebele (closest to the light sage green pearl) and the row below that row. Using the second row down as your working row, do 1 round, adding 2 teal 24-karat-lined 15°s between each of the 4 beads to create 4 ladders of Ndebele. Step up at the end of this round (figure 1).

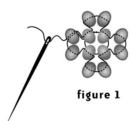

figure 1

2 Do another round of teal 24-karat-lined 15°s, this time adding 2 beads on each ladder and 1 bead in between each ladder. Step up at the end of this round (figure 2).

3 Stitch 1 round of Ndebele in matte metallic blue-purple 15°s, doing a 2-bead stitch on each of the 4 ladders of Ndebele, and adding 2 beads between each ladder (figure 3).

4 Step up and do another round of Ndebele using matte metallic blue-purple 15°s. This time add 2 beads on top of each of the 4 original ladders and also on top of each of the 4 newly formed ladders between each of the original ladders (figure 4).

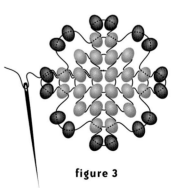

figure 2

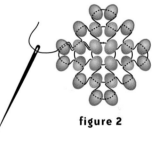

figure 3

5 Weave 9 more rows of 8-ladder tubular Ndebele (6 in matte metallic blue purple 15°s, and 3 in bright blue-purple semi-matte gilt lined). Do a final row adding one 15° Czech charlotte on each ladder and 1 magatama between each ladder, to create the flared effect at the base of the bell.

▶ Assembly

1 Attach an ear wire to the loop of 15° charlottes at the top of the earrings. To do so, pry open the loop on the ear wire with chain-nose pliers. Slip the loop of beads onto the ear wire, then close the ear wire.

2 Repeat to make a second earring.

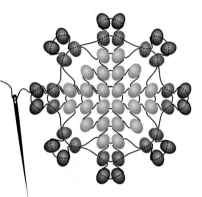

figure 4

Laura McCabe

Beetlewing Choker, 2009

20.3 x 25.4 x 6.4 cm

Glass seed beads, custom-cut green goldstone points by Gary Wilson lapidary, crystal beads, beetle wings, suede, 14-karat gold slide clasp; peyote stitch, embellishment, branch fringe

PHOTO BY MELINDA HOLDEN

SUPPLIES

Basic Beading Kit (page 12)

Size 11° Japanese
cylinder beads:

Opaque blue luster, 1 g

Shiny opaque black, 1 g

Size 11° Japanese seed beads:

Matte metallic
medium-blue, 10 g

Matte opaque black, 10 g

Size 15° Japanese seed beads:

Shiny opaque black, 10 g

Opaque blue luster, 1 g

4 freshwater potato pearls,
5–6 mm

315* Czech daggers, 5 x 16 mm

*Quantity required for a 7-inch
(17.8 cm) bracelet. The design
calls for 45 daggers per 1 inch
(2.5 cm) of spiral.

NUDIBRANCH
BRACELET

This densely embellished bracelet illustrates how a basic spiral rope

combined with a simple ornamental form can create a piece with the flowing

structure of a nudibranch, a marine creature (see page 53)—and a bracelet with

wonderful visual appeal.

▶ Spiral Rope Base

The spiral rope base is made using 11° seed beads for the core and outer beads. Instructions for the basic spiral rope weave appear on page 20.

For the piece shown here, I used matte metallic medium-blue 11°s for the core and matte opaque black 11°s for the outer beads of the spiral. When the bracelet is completed, the spiral base is completely embellished and barely visible.

1 Begin by single threading approximately 10 feet (3 m) of beading thread on a size 12 beading needle. Wax well. Leave a 12-inch (30.5 cm) tail to use later for attaching the clasp. Weave a section of spiral rope approximately the desired length of the finished bracelet (figures 1 and 2); although the toggle closure adds length, the thickness of the embellishment will cause the inner diameter of the bracelet to shrink, effectively reducing the length of the base spiral rope. It's important to consider this during construction.

figure 1

▶ Clasp

The clasp is a beaded toggle closure, composed of a beaded toggle ring and a beaded toggle bar with connector tabs, described on pages 24 and 25.

1 Construct the toggle ring using shiny opaque black 15°s and opaque blue luster cylinder beads. Use thirty-six 15°s to begin the ring. Once the ring is complete, embellish the middle row of cylinder beads with 1 matte opaque 11° between every bead along the row. Complete the toggle ring by adding the connector tab, following the instructions on page 24. Embellish the connector tab on each side with shiny opaque black 15°s.

2 Make the toggle bar using shiny opaque black cylinder beads with opaque blue luster 15°s. Use shiny opaque black 15°s to attach pearls at either end of the bar. Complete the toggle bar by adding the connector tab. Embellish the connector tab on each side with opaque blue luster 15°s.

figure 2

▶ Attach the Closure

You're ready to attach the clasp components to each end of the bracelet.

1 Using the tail thread at the end of your spiral rope, pick up one end bead—a potato pearl. Thread up 19 shiny opaque black 15° seed beads. Slide the connector loop on the toggle ring or toggle bar over the 15°s. Go back through the pearl and down through 3 core beads in the spiral.

2 Pick up 3 of the outer spiral beads— matte opaque black 11°s—and pass through the pearl, through the loop of 15°s (which are going through the toggle connector loop), back down through the pearl, and down through 2 core beads in the spiral.

3 Pick up 2 of the outer spiral beads and pass through the pearl, through the loop of 15°s, back down through the pearl, and down through 1 core bead in the spiral.

4 Pick up 1 of the outer spiral beads and pass through the pearl, through the loop of 15°s, back down through the pearl, and into the core beads. Knot off the thread by half hitching 2 or 3 times in the outer spiral beads before weaving in the tail and cutting it off.

5 Repeat the same attachment method at the other end of the spiral using the other component of the toggle closure.

▶ Embellish the Spiral Rope

Dagger fringe embellishments marvelously mimic the bushy extremities on nudibranch backs. They're woven into the spiral rope base between each core bead. I generally use a doubled thread when embellishing a piece of beadwork like this one that will get a lot of wear and tear.

1 Thread up 15 feet (4.6 m) of thread on a size 12 English beading needle. Double and wax the thread.

2 Weave into the spiral rope near one end, half hitching twice within the outer spiral beads, and work your way toward the end of the spiral rope to come out between the last and next-to-last core beads.

3 Pick up one 11°, four 15°s, 1 dagger, and four 15°s. Go back through the 11° and into the second core bead in the spiral.

4 Coming out of the second core bead, pick up two 11°s, four 15°s, 1 dagger, and four 15°s. Go back through the second 11° you picked up. Pick up four 15°s, 1 dagger, and four 15°s, and go back through the first 11° you picked up and back into the third core bead on the spiral.

5 Coming out of the third core bead, pick up three 11°s, four 15°s, 1 dagger, and four 15°s. Go back through the third 11° you picked up (figure 3). Pick up four 15°s, 1 dagger, and four 15°s, then go back through the second 11° you picked up (figure 4). Pick up four 15°s, 1 dagger, and four 15°s; go back through the first 11° you picked up and back into the fourth core bead on the spiral (figure 5).

6 Continue in this manner, adding 3-dagger fringe all the way along the spiral until you reach the third-to-last 11° bead in the spiral rope core at the other end. (You'll need to

add thread at various points during the embellishment process. Half hitch old threads off twice between outer spiral beads and then weave in the tail and cut. Add new threads in the same manner as you did with the first embellishment thread.)

7 When you're exiting from the third-to-last 11° in the core, add a 2-dagger fringe. Between the second-to-last and the last 11° in the core, add a 1-dagger fringe to taper off the end.

8 Weave in all threads and half hitch twice before cutting the tails.

figure 3

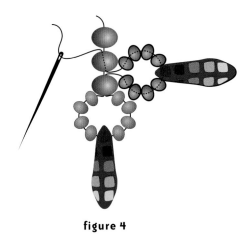

figure 4

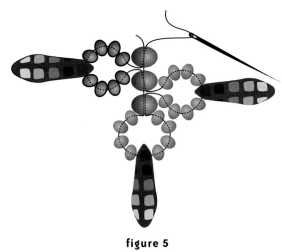

figure 5

SUPPLIES

Basic Beading Kit (page 12)

Size 11° Japanese
cylinder beads:

    Light green and/or yellow
    dichroic Aikos, 4 g

    Metallic blue, 10 g

Size 11° Japanese seed beads:

    Matte opaque black, 15 g

    Chartreuse gilt lined, 3 g

Size 15° Japanese seed beads:

    Teal gilt lined, 3 g

    Root beer gold luster, 3 g

24-karat-gold-plated size
15° Czech charlottes, 3 g

10 orange freshwater
pearls, 6 mm

8 peacock blue freshwater
pearls, 5 mm

Approx. 50 jet AB2X crystal
bicones, 3 mm

Approx. 144 mixed aqua
and blue opal round
crystal beads, 2 mm

4 flat, round Czech glass spacer
beads, 12 mm

86

CHERRY BLOSSOM
PENDANT NECKLACE

By adding floral embellishments to an irregularly shaped flat peyote stitch base,
you create a beautiful focal point for the necklace. The necklace strap
integrates beaded beads, Czech glass spacer beads, and pearls with Ndebele.

Note: Japanese charlottes are *much* larger than Czech charlottes; the two are not interchangeable. Be sure to use the type described in the materials list.

Pendant

▶ Peyote Base

Refer to figure 1 as you work.

1 Add 1 g of dichroic Aikos 11ºs to the 10 g of metallic blue cylinder beads to create the bead mix for the peyote base. Single thread approximately 10 feet (3 m) on a beading needle and wax it well. Leave a tail 6 feet (1.8 m) long (you'll use this later to weave the bottom half of the pendant base) and begin weaving a strip of flat, even-count peyote with cylinder beads 20 beads wide by 26 rows long (count 13 beads up either side). Refer to page 17 for instructions on flat, even-count peyote.

2 For the next row, decrease on each side by 4 beads. The peyote strip is now only 12 beads wide. Weave a tab that's 24 rows long (count 12 beads up each side). Zip this last row to the first row with 12 cylinder beads across to create a bail. Picot each side of the bail with 15° charlottes.

3 Go back to the other side of the 20-bead-wide tab and thread up the tail onto a size 12 English beading needle. Decrease the width of the new row you're adding by 4 beads on the left side (bottom side of figure 1), and weave a total of 3 rows 16 beads wide.

4 Decrease the width of the next row by 4 beads on the right side (top side of figure 1) and weave 10 rows 12 beads wide.

5 Decrease the width of the next row on both sides by 4 beads and weave 8 rows 4 beads wide.

6 Decrease the width of the row by 1 bead on each side and weave a tab 24 rows long by 2 beads wide. Don't zip this tab; it will be zipped to form a loop in a later step.

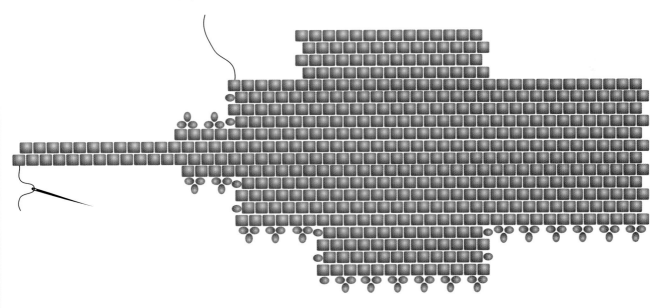

figure 1

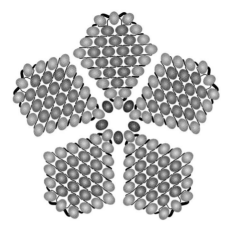

figure 2

figure 3

▶ Cherry Blossom Flowers

The cherry blossom flowers featured in the pendant are made using the technique described on page 38. Make 2. As shown here, 1 flower is made of root beer gold luster 15°s; the other uses teal gilt-lined 15°s (figure 2).

▶ Rings

1 The basic ring form is created using size 15° teal gilt-lined round seed beads and dichroic Aikos size 11° cylinder beads. Following the directions given on page 23, make 2 beaded rings using thirty-six 15°s for the initial circle of beads. Set 1 ring aside (tails left on) to make into the toggle ring later.

2 On the second ring, add 1 chartreuse gilt-lined 11° between every cylinder bead along the center row of cylinder beads around the outside of the ring. Weave off the tails. This ring in now ready to be added to the pendant (figure 3).

▶ Assemble and Embellish the Pendant

1 With the base now complete, slide the ring onto the long 2-bead-wide tab at the bottom of the peyote pendant base piece and zip the tab to itself—zipping the last row of the tab to the first row of the tab—to add the ring as a free-swinging component at the base of the pendant.

2 Edge the entire base, including the bottom tab and the top bail, with 15° charlotte picots.

3 Attach the cherry blossoms to the front side of the pendant base in a random pattern using an 11°, an orange pearl, and a 3-bead 15° charlotte picot. Coming out of the flat peyote surface, pick up one 11°, the beaded cherry blossom (face up), an orange pearl, and three 15° charlottes. Go back down through the pearl and the 11° (the 15° charlottes form a picot), and weave back into the peyote base (figure 4).

4 Embellish the space between, and the area surrounding, the cherry blossoms with branch fringe tipped with a contrasting 11°, a 3mm bicone, and three 15° Czech charlottes, following the directions on page 43 (figure 5). I usually add 6 or more of these in a random pattern to the peyote pendant base.

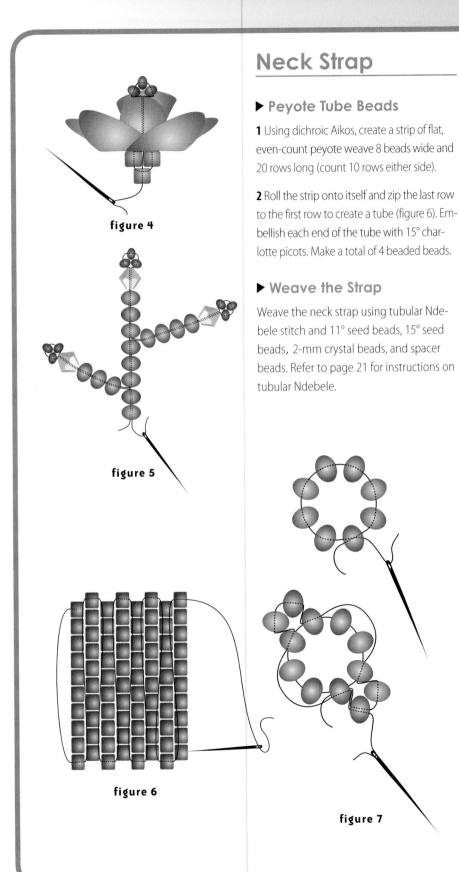

figure 4

figure 5

figure 6

figure 7

Neck Strap

▶ Peyote Tube Beads

1 Using dichroic Aikos, create a strip of flat, even-count peyote weave 8 beads wide and 20 rows long (count 10 rows either side).

2 Roll the strip onto itself and zip the last row to the first row to create a tube (figure 6). Embellish each end of the tube with 15° charlotte picots. Make a total of 4 beaded beads.

▶ Weave the Strap

Weave the neck strap using tubular Ndebele stitch and 11° seed beads, 15° seed beads, 2-mm crystal beads, and spacer beads. Refer to page 21 for instructions on tubular Ndebele.

1 Thread a size 13 beading needle with approximately 2 wingspans of thread and wax well. Working with a single thread, and leaving a tail at least 16 inches (40.6 cm) long, pick up 8 matte black opaque 11° round beads. Circle around and go back through the first 11° to form a circle.

2 Pick up two 11°s and go through the very next bead in the circle. Skip over the next 2 beads in the circle and go through the bead after that.

3 Again, pick up two 11°s and go through the very next bead in the circle. Skip over the next two beads in the circle and go through the bead after that. The bead you've just gone through should be the bead the original tail is exiting from (figure 7).

4 Step up through the next bead and pull—the 2 ladders should take form, creating a tube of Ndebele that already has 3 rows. You're ready to begin normal tubular Ndebele stitch (with a step up at the end of each round) using a mixture of 2-mm crystals and size 11° seed beads. Mix the crystal beads in at random to add sparkle to the weave. Do a total of 12 rows (including the 3 row start). Then do 3 rows with root beer gold luster 15°s.

Add the beaded bead in the following manner:

5 Pick up a blue pearl, about eight 11°s (and slide the beaded bead over them), another blue pearl, and two root beer gold luster 15°s. Go back through the pearl, the 11°s (within the peyote tube), the pearl, and down into the second 15° in the first ladder of Ndebele. Come up through the first bead in the second ladder of Ndebele, go through the pearl, the 11°s (within the peyote tube), and the pearl. Add 2 more 15°s. Go back down through the pearl, the 11°s (within the peyote tube) and the pearl, and into the second bead in the second ladder of Ndebele. Turn around and come up through the first bead in the first ladder, up through the pearl, the 11°s (within the peyote tube), the pearl, and 1 of the 15°s on top. Use these 15°s to resume the Ndebele stitch.

6 Do 2 more rows using root beer gold luster 15°s (for a total of 3 rows of 15°s), followed by 16 rows using a combination of 2-mm crystals and size 11° seed beads. Then do 3 rows of teal gilt-lined 15°s.

Add the spacer beads in the following manner:

7 Pick up an orange pearl, a spacer bead, an orange pearl, and two teal gilt-lined 15°s. Go back through the pearl, the spacer bead, the pearl, and down into the second 15° in the first ladder of Ndebele. Come up through the first bead in the second ladder of Ndebele, go through the pearl, the 11°s, and the pearl. Add two more teal gilt-lined 15°s. Go back down through the pearl, the spacer bead, and the pearl, and into the second bead in the second ladder of Ndebele. Turn around and come up through the first bead in the first ladder, up through the pearl, the 11°s, the spacer bead, and 1 of the 15°s on top. Resume Ndebele stitch. Do two more rows of teal gilt-lined 15°s, for a total of 3 rows.

8 Do 16 rows using a combination of 2-mm crystals and matte black opaque size 11° seed beads, and then 3 rows using 15°s. Add a pearl, peyote tube, and pearl (following the instructions outlined above in step 5), followed by the 3 rows of root beer gold luster 15°s.

9 Bead 16 rows of a combination of 2-mm crystals and size 11° seed beads.

10 Next, add the pendant: Pick up an orange pearl, a spacer bead, and two 11°s. Go back through the spacer bead, the pearl, and down into the second 11° in the first ladder of Ndebele. Come up through the first bead in the second ladder of Ndebele, go through the pearl and the spacer bead, and add 2 more 11°s. Go back down through the spacer bead, the pearl, and into the second bead in the second ladder of Ndebele. Turn around and come up through the first bead in the first ladder, through the pearl, the spacer bead, and 1 of the 11°s on top.

11 Resume Ndebele stitch, adding 9 more rows, using size 11° seed beads.

12 Slide the bail of the embellished peyote pendant over the just-stitched rows of Ndebele and hold it snug against the spacer bead. If necessary, do extra rows so the end of the tube is in line with the edge of the bail. Now pick up a spacer bead, an orange pearl, and two 11°s. Go back through the pearl, the spacer bead, and down into the second 11° in the first ladder of Ndebele. Come up through the first bead in the second ladder of Ndebele, go through the spacer bead, the pearl, and add 2 more 11°s. Go back down through the pearl, the spacer bead, and into the second bead in the second ladder of Ndebele. Turn around and come up through the first bead in the first ladder, through the spacer bead, the pearl, and 1 of the 11°s on top.

13 Resume Ndebele stitch, adding 15 more rows (1 row was already added at the top of the pearl) using matte opaque black 11°s with occasional 2-mm crystals.

14 Add 3 rows of root beer gold luster 15°s and a beaded bead (following the instructions outlined above), followed by a total of 3 more rows of root beer gold luster 15°s and 16 rows of 11° seed beads (with occasional 2-mm crystals). Then do 3 rows of teal gilt-lined 15°s. Add a spacer bead (following the instructions outlined above).

15 Bead a total of 3 more rows of root beer gold luster 15°s after the beaded bead and then do 12 rows of 11° seed beads with occasional 2-mm crystals (figure 8).

▶ Toggle Closure

By using both the ring form and peyote tube bead form described on page 23, you can make an attractive closure that's consistent with the overall piece.

Toggle Loop

The ring portion of the toggle loop is already made; it's the ring set aside earlier when you constructed 2 rings in the Rings section on page 88.

1 Add the connector loop to the ring. Working off of the middle row of cylinder beads, use the working thread from the ring to add 20 rows (count 10 rows up either side) of 2-bead peyote stitch using dichroic Aikos 11° cylinder beads; zip the last row to the first row of the 2-bead strip to form the connector loop. Edge each side of the connector loop with 15° charlotte picots. Add 1 chartreuse gilt-lined 11° between every bead along the middle row of cylinder beads of the ring form.

Toggle Bar

1 Pick up 14 cylinder beads to begin a strip of even-count peyote stitch 14 beads wide by 12 rows long (count 6 beads up each side). Zip the first row to the last row to form a tube. Embellish each end of the bar with an orange pearl and add a connector tab, following the directions on page 25.

Attach the toggle closure by threading up the tail at the end of the neck strap. Coming out of the first bead in the first ladder of Ndebele, pick up 19 size 15° seed beads. Go through the connector loop on the toggle (ring or bar) and then back down into the second bead in the first ladder of Ndebele. Turn around and come up through the first bead in the second ladder of Ndebele, through all the 15°s in the

loop of beads, and down into the second bead in the second ladder of Ndebele. Weave off the tail within the neck strap. Repeat this procedure on the other end of the neck strap to attach the second half of the toggle closure.

figure 8

91

SUPPLIES

Basic Beading Kit (page 12)

Size 11° Japanese seed beads:

    Chartreuse gilt lined, 2 g

    Metallic dark plum, 2 g

Size 15° Japanese seed beads:

    Chartreuse gold lined, 1 g

    Matte metallic olive gold, 1 g

    Aqua plum lined, 1 g

    Metallic dark plum, 1 g

    Metallic dark purple, 1 g

6 yellow freshwater pearls, 5.5 mm

4 or more magenta freshwater pearls, 4 mm

Matte metallic dark plum 3-mm Japanese magatamas, 4 g

25 or more Czech glass drops, 4 x 6 mm

2 Czech faceted rondelles, 4 x 6 mm

French ear wires, 1 pair

Chain-nose pliers

STAR FLOWER EARRINGS

These floral-inspired earrings incorporate a range of embellishment techniques, including basic bud forms, berry cluster forms, and star flowers. For a gorgeous-looking set, whip them up in colors that complement the Eye Flower Pendant Necklace on page 94.

1 Cut 15 feet (4.6 m) or so of thread, thread it onto a size 12 beading needle, and double it. Wax it well.

2 Thread one 11° seed bead; slide it down, leaving about 10 inches (25.4 cm) of tail, and circle back through the bead to create a stop bead. String on 14 to 16 chartreuse gilt-lined 11° seed beads. The more beads you use, the larger the overall size of the earring. You'll begin at the bottom of the form and work your way up toward the ear wire, embellishing as you go.

▶ Star Flower

1 Pick up 1 yellow pearl and three 15°s in an A–B–A color sequence, with chartreuse gilt lined as color A, and matte metallic olive gold as color B. Go back through the pearl to create a picot of 15°s.

2 Pick up nine 15°s in a B–A–B–A–B–A–B–A–B color sequence. Go through all 3 beads in the picot. Pick up 9 more 15°s in a B–A–B–A–B–A–B–A–B color sequence. Pass through the bottommost 11° (on the stalk) toward the pearl.

3 Go through the first 15° in the circle of beads around the pearl; it should be a B-colored bead. Begin peyote stitching (page 17) with C-colored 15°s. (Color C is aqua plum lined.) When you reach the picot, pass through just the middle bead, and continue peyote stitching around the other side. When you reach the stalk, pass through the bottommost 11° toward the pearl, and step up through the B bead from the first round and the C bead from the last round. You're ready to add petals between each of these C beads.

4 Coming out of the first C bead, pick up one 15° in color D, 1 metallic dark plum 11°, and three 15°s in color E. (Color D is metallic dark plum and E is metallic dark purple.) Go back through the 11° to form a picot of E-colored 15°s. Pick up 1 more D-colored 15° and go through the next C bead. Repeat this process 8 more times, creating a total of 9 petals. Once you've gone though the last C bead, finishing the ninth petal, pass through a B-colored 15° and down through the second-to-last 11° in the stalk. At this point, the last 11° in the stalk has been totally incorporated into the flower form, so you won't need to pass through it (figure 1). For more information on Star Flower construction, refer to page 32.

▶ **Embellish**

1 Add several embellishments to the stalk between this first completed star flower and the area where you'll add the next flower. To do so, add 5 to 7 embellishments, 1 between each 11°. These can be simple bud embellishments (page 27) made with 4-mm pearls (figure 2) or berry clusters (page 30) made with magatamas and Czech drops (figure 3). The berry clusters can vary in length from one 11° with 1 drop to three 11°s with 3 drops.

2 Coming off of the main stalk, pick up 3 or 4 size 11°s and construct a second star flower as described previously. Next, travel back through the branch of 11°s to the main stalk and resume embellishing—with pearls or berry clusters—for 3 or 4 more beads.

3 Branch out again to create the third star flower. Pick up 3 or 4 size 11°s and construct the third star flower, then travel back through the branch of 11°s to the main stalk and resume embellishing—with pearls or berry clusters—all the way to the top, with the last embellishment falling between the second and the first 11°.

▶ **Finish Off**

1 Unthread the tails from the stop bead and thread up both tails onto a single needle. Using this threaded tail, pick up 1 rondelle, one 4-mm pearl, and nine 15° seed beads. Go back through the pearl and rondelle and weave off the tail, half hitching a couple of times between 11° stalk beads (figure 4).

2 Pass the working thread up through the rondelle, the pearl, the nine 15°s, and back down through the pearl and the rondelle and weave off this tail, half hitching a couple of times. Cut off all tail threads.

3 Attach an ear wire to the loop of 15°s at the top of the earring. Do so by prying open the loop on the ear wire with chain-nose pliers. Slip the loop of beads onto the ear wire, then close the ear wire.

4 Repeat to make a second earring. You don't have to strive for symmetry; differences simply reinforce the organic feel.

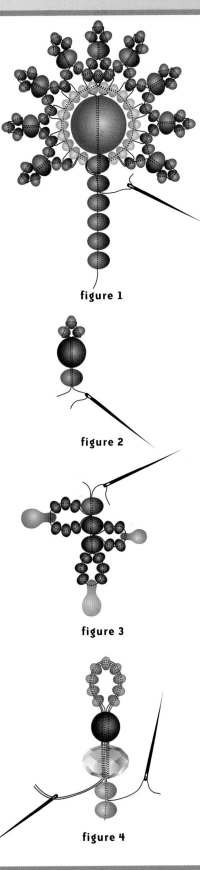

figure 1

figure 2

figure 3

figure 4

EYE FLOWER PENDANT NECKLACE

Capture a cabochon with a beaded bezel, and embellish it to create a wonderful floral pendant necklace.

Note: Japanese charlottes are *much* larger than Czech charlottes; the two are not interchangeable. Be sure to use the type described in the materials list.

▶ Bezel the Cabochon

1 Glue the cabochon to a piece of leather about ½-inch (1.3 cm) larger than the stone on all sides. Using a toothpick, apply an even coat of adhesive to the back of the cabochon. Place the glue-covered side of the cabochon down on the right side (the smooth side) of the leather, making sure you maintain about a ½-inch (1.3 cm) border of leather around the perimeter of the stone. Allow to dry for at least 10 minutes.

2 Sew the bezel's foundation row of beads along the perimeter of the cabochon. Single thread approximately 6 feet (1.8 m) on a size 12 beading needle, and wax well. Tie a knot at the end and cut, leaving a ¼-inch (6 mm) tail. Pass the needle up through the leather from the back side, coming up next to the cabochon. Pull the thread tight so the knot is snug against the leather.

3 String on 6 chartreuse gold-lined cylinder beads, slide the beads down the thread to the edge of the cabochon, arrange them in a line closely against the stone, and stitch back down through the leather at the end of the line formed by the beads. Sew back up through the leather with the needle coming through the leather between the third and fourth bead, then pass through beads 4, 5, and 6 again—creating an embroidery backstitch (figure 1). Continue this 6-bead embroidery backstitch around the perimeter of the stone. As you finish this row make sure the row contains an even number of beads; if necessary, adjust the number of beads in the final stitch to accomplish this. Travel through this row of beads one more time, to ensure good tension.

figure 1

SUPPLIES

Basic Beading Kit (page 12)

1 eye agate cabochon, 16–25 mm

Size 11° Japanese cylinder beads:

> **Chartreuse gold lined, 3 g**
>
> **Metallic dark purple, 1 g**

Size 11° Japanese seed beads:

> **Chartreuse gold lined, 5 g**
>
> **Metallic dark plum, 5 g**
>
> **Aqua plum lined, 3 g**

Size 15° Japanese seed beads:

> **Metallic dark purple, 10 g**
>
> **Aqua plum lined, 3 g**
>
> **Metallic dark plum, 1 g**
>
> **Chartreuse gold lined, 1 g**
>
> **Matte metallic olive gold, 3 g**
>
> **Metallic purple, 1 g**

Size 15° Czech charlottes:

> **Bronze, 1 g**
>
> **Marcasite, 1 g**

10+ gold-colored freshwater pearls, 5.5 mm

10+ magenta freshwater pearls, 4 mm

50+ fuchsia Czech glass drops, 4 x 6 mm

Matte metallic dark plum 3-mm Japanese magatamas, 3 g

Leather, 2 pieces, each approximately 1 1/2 inches (3.8 cm) square

Adhesive and toothpicks

4 Begin peyote stitching upward from the base row: Pick up a bead, skip a bead, go through a bead (figure 2). Continue peyote stitching with cylinder beads for a couple of rows until you reach the curve in the cabochon (the number of rows will vary with the thickness of the cabochon). There should be at least 3 rows of cylinder beads (including the row of embroidery that has now transformed into peyote). When the cabochon starts to curve in, switch to size 15°s; the decrease in bead size will cause the bezel to curve inward, creating a tight fit against the cabochon. Stitch 2 rows of 15°s. Pull each bead tightly into place. The cabochon should be securely held by the bezel. If not, you may need to add another 1 or 2 rows of 15°s. The final row should be done in bronze 15° Czech charlottes. Again, pull each bead tightly into place. (**Note**: The row count for both cylinder beads and 15°s will vary depending on the height of your cab.)

5 Weave the thread back through the beads to the base row and pass through the leather. Come back up through the leather next to the outside of the foundation row of the beaded bezel. Backstitch 1 more row of chartreuse gold-lined cylinder beads (6 at a time, as before), placing the beads snug alongside the foundation row. As you finish this row, make sure it contains an even number of beads; if necessary, adjust the number of beads in the final stitch to accomplish this. Pass through this row a couple of times to straighten up the row of beads. Weave through to the back side, knot off, and cut the thread.

▶ Embellish and Add Petals

1 Cut 10 feet (3 m) of thread and double thread a needle. Knot the end, leaving a tail ¼ inch (6 mm) long. Needle up from the back side of the leather into the peyote bezel. Travel up to the topmost row of cylinder beads in the bezel and stitch 1 row, adding 1 chartreuse gold-lined 11° between the beads that form the topmost row (figure 3).

2 Weave down a row and stitch a row, adding 3 marcasite 15° Czech charlottes between each bead in the row to create picots. Weave down a row and do a second row of picots, adding 3 marcasite 15° Czech charlottes between every bead in the row (figure 4).

3 You're ready to embellish the bezel with pointed peyote flower petals. Weave down 1 row in the bezel and come out between the cylinder beads. String on 1 metallic dark plum 11° and nine 15°s, 6 of color A—metallic dark purple—and three of color B—aqua plum lined. Double back through the sixth 15° to create a picot (figure 5).

4 Peyote stitch toward the bezel with color A beads (figure 6). Turn around and peyote stitch with color A beads around the petal 1 more time to create a nice petal shape. As you peyote stitch this round, stitch the sides of the petal with color A beads, switch to a color B bead immediately before the picot, pass through the picot, and add another color B to maintain the contrasting-color petal tip, then switch back to color A beads to complete the second side of the petal. When you've finished 1 petal, pass through the 11° at the base of the petal and stitch through the next bead in the bezel and repeat until petals are added

all of the way around the bezel (figure 7). For more detailed instructions on pointed peyote petals, see page 33.

5 After finishing the row of petals, weave down through the bezel beads and knot off on the back side of the leather.

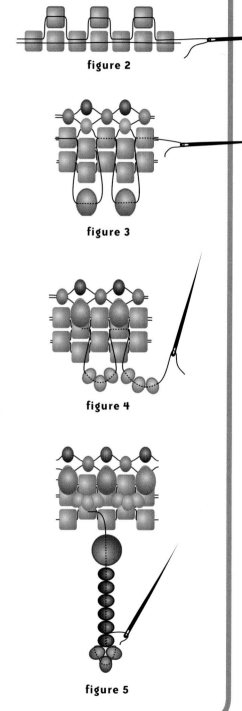

figure 2

figure 3

figure 4

figure 5

▶ Back the Cabochon and Finish Its Edges

1 Cut 6 feet (1.8 m) of nylon thread in a color that matches your leather, single thread it, and knot the end as before. Pass the thread up through the leather, coming out between the bezel and the beads in the outer base row.

2 Using a toothpick, apply adhesive to the back side of the leather, taking care not to smear any on the thread hanging from the front side. Place the second piece of leather on the back of the cabochon, right side (smooth side) out, and press to ensure evenness. Allow to dry for at least 10 minutes.

3 Cut away the excess leather, leaving a small edge about the width of a row of cylinder beads. Using the thread already attached to the piece, pass the needle through both pieces of leather to the back side and overhand stitch the entire perimeter of the piece. This helps ensure the backing won't come off, and gives a nice finished look to the piece.

4 Pass the needle back up through both pieces of leather and through a couple beads in the outer base row. Begin peyote stitching outward to cover up the leather edge. Do 1 row of metallic dark purple cylinder beads and 2 rows of 11°s—first row, metallic dark plum; second row, chartreuse gold lined.

▶ Bail

1 After completing the outer rows, weave the thread up to the top of the cabochon. Begin to flat, even count peyote stitch a strip 6 to 8 beads wide. This will create a tab that will be looped around and attached to itself to create a bail (figure 8). The tab should be at least 28 rows long (count 14 beads up each side) in order to fit around the spiral rope neck strap. After the tab is stitched to length, fold it over and zip it to itself, zipping the last row to the first. Add Czech charlotte picots along each side of the bail (figure 9).

▶ Neck Strap

1 The neck strap for this necklace is created using a variation on basic spiral rope (page 20). This variation is constructed using both 11°s and 15°s. The core beads are chartreuse gold-lined 11°s. The outer bead sequence is 1 aqua plum lined 15°, 1 metallic dark purple 15°, 1 metallic dark plum 11°, 1 metallic dark purple 15°, and 1 aqua plum-lined 15°.

2 Build your spiral 1½ inches (3.8 cm) shorter than the desired length of the finished piece (the toggle closure will add the additional length to the strap).

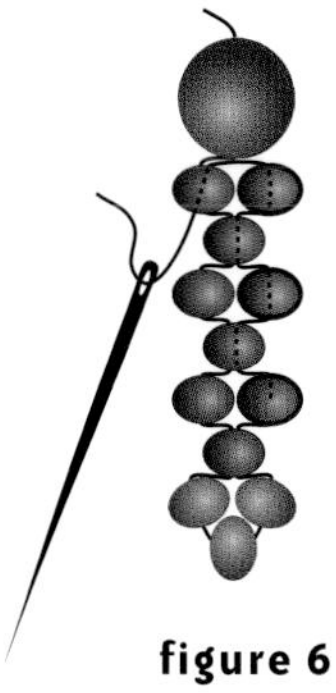

figure 6

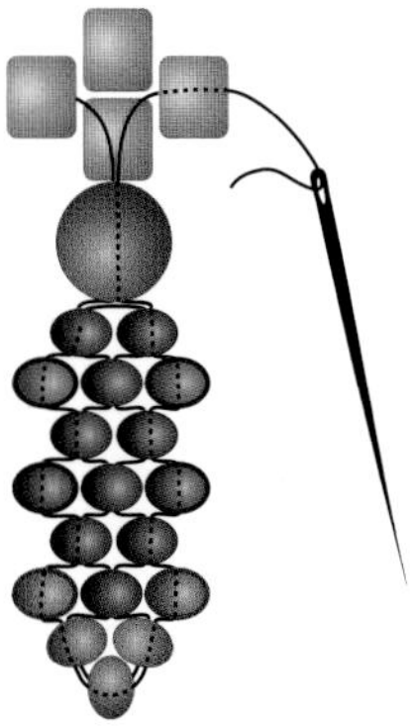

figure 7

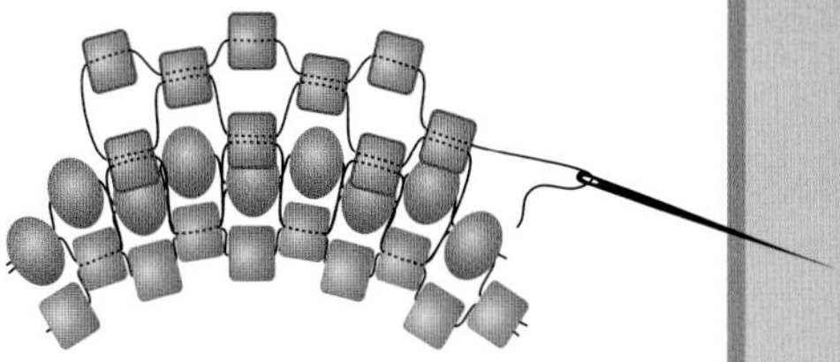

figure 8

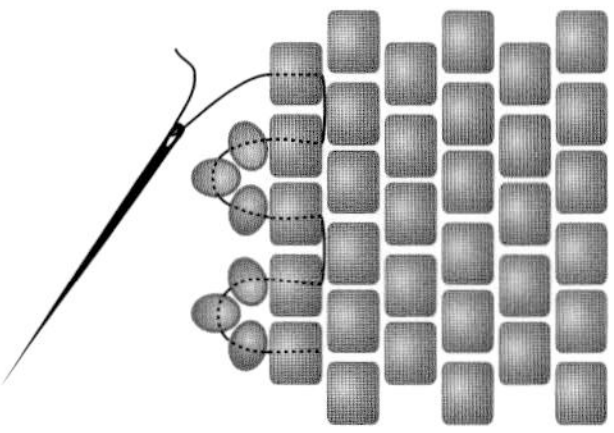

figure 9

▶ Embellish the Neck Strap

The embellishments at the center front of the necklace are a random collection of the following embellishment forms:

- **Star Flower** (page 32), using yellow pearls, 11°s, and 15°s

- **Berry Cluster** (page 30), using Czech drops, magatamas, 11°s, and 15°s (figure 10)

- **Simple Bud and Bud Branching**. This simplified version of the Flower Cluster on page 29 uses magenta pearls, 11°s, and 15°s (figure 11).

1 Find the center of the neck strap and begin adding embellishment forms, starting about 1 inch (2.5 cm) off of center and working toward the center. After embellishing about ⅝ inch (1.6 cm) of the spiral, weave the working thread through the core beads for a distance equal to or slightly greater than the width of the cabochon bail. This area of the spiral rope will be covered by the bail. Then slide the finished pendant over the spiral rope and embellish about ⅝ inch (1.6 cm) of the spiral rope this side of the bail. After embellishing, weave in the tail, half hitching a couple of times before cutting the thread.

▶ Toggle Closure

1 For instructions on making a beaded toggle closure, refer to pages 24 and 25. For this project, metallic dark purple cylinder beads were used in the toggle ring and chartreuse gold-lined cylinder beads were used in the toggle bar to create color contrast in the closure.

2 When the toggle components are complete, attach the toggle ring to one of the ends of the spiral rope. Using the thread emerging from the end of the spiral, pick up 1 yellow pearl, 1 magenta pearl, and 21 marcasite 15° charlottes. Slide the connector loop on the toggle ring over these 21 beads, then go back through the pearls and down through 3 core beads in the spiral rope (figure 12).

3 Pick up 4 outer-color beads (1 aqua plum-lined 15°, 1 metallic dark purple 15°, 1 metallic dark plum 11°, and 1 metallic dark purple 15°) and go back up through the pearls, the 21 charlottes, back down through the pearls, and down through 2 core beads in the spiral rope (figure 13).

4 Pick up 3 outer-color beads (1 aqua plum-lined 15°, 1 metallic dark purple 15°, and 1 metallic dark plum 11°) and go back up through the pearls, pick up 21 marcasite 15° charlottes, and go through the connector loop on the toggle. Go back down through the pearls, and down through 1 core bead in the spiral rope (figure 14).

5 Pick up 2 outer-color beads (1 aqua plum-lined 15°, 1 metallic dark purple 15°) and go back up through the pearls, through the second set of twenty-one 15° charlottes, back down through the pearls, and down through 1 core bead. Tie off this thread within the spiral (figure 15).

6 Repeat the same procedure at the other end of the spiral with the toggle bar.

figure 12

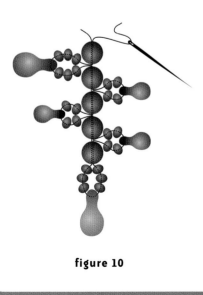

figure 10

figure 11

98

figure 13

figure 14

figure 15

Laura McCabe
Lisa Niven Kelly

Party Necklace, 2005

Length, 48.3 cm; centerpiece, 5.1 x 7.6 cm

Vintage crystal stones, crystal sequins and beads,
sterling silver wire, glass seed beads; peyote stitch,
wire work, embellishment

PHOTO BY MELINDA HOLDEN

KESHI PEARL NECKLACE

This necklace was designed to provide a lesson in embellishing spiral rope with a variety of forms. A combination of floral and marine designs inspired me. The project also incorporates a tidy way to finish off spiral ropes with a button closure.

▶ Spiral Rope Base

The base of this necklace is made from 11° and 15° Japanese seed beads woven into a spiral rope, which is described on page 20. Using a single threaded size 12 English beading needle, weave a section of spiral rope that is approximately 2 inches (5.1 cm) shorter than your desired finished necklace length. Use metallic dark plum 11°s as the core beads and two 15°s (first a chartreuse gold-lined 15°, then a root beer gold luster 15°), 1 root beer gold luster 11°, and two 15°s (first a root beer gold luster 15°, then a chartreuse gold-lined 15°) for the outer sequence.

Note: To save time, you can also weave spiral rope using metallic dark plum 11°s for the core and 3 root beer gold luster 11°s for the outer sequence. Either way, the spiral base will be completely embellished and barely visible when the necklace is completed.

▶ Clasp

Use a new or vintage button to create a beautiful and unusual closure. The finishing technique described here allows you to attach the button closure while simultaneously finishing off the spiral rope with a neat, tapered-off end.

1 Using the tail thread at the end of your spiral rope, pick up 3 end beads—a 4 x 8-mm faceted glass rondelle, a 4 x 6-mm rondelle, and a 2 x 4-mm rondelle. Then pick up six 11° seed beads, a 2 x 4-mm rondelle, and three 15°s. Slide on the button so the shank slides up and over the 15°s. Pick up another 2 x 4-mm rondelle (to keep the button from sliding around) and 6 more 11°s. Pass back down through the end beads and through 3 of the core beads in the spiral rope (figure 1).

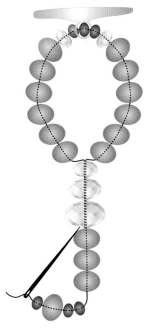

figure 1

SUPPLIES

Basic Beading Kit (page 12)

Size 11° Japanese seed beads:
   Metallic dark plum, 10 g
   Root beer gold luster, 20 g

Size 15° Japanese seed beads:
   Chartreuse gold lined, 10 g
   Root beer gold luster, 10 g
   Metallic dark plum, 5 g
   Periwinkle gilt lined, 5 g
   Aqua bright pink lined, 5 g

A variety of freshwater pearls:
   Mostly keshi (about two
   16-inch [40.6 cm] strands)

A few potato pearls (used in the center of the star flowers)

A variety of other glass beads, including leaves, flowers, crystal bicones etc. (used as various embellishments throughout the central cluster)

3-mm magatamas, 20 grams mixed with about 100 4 x 6-mm Czech drops

Faceted glass rondelles:
   2 opaline glass, 4 x 8 mm
   2 opaline glass, 4 x 6 mm
   Approximately 60 opaline glass, 2 x 4 mm

1 round button, 16 mm

figure 2

figure 3

figure 4

2 Still referring to figure 1, turn around and pick up 4 outer-color beads (1 chartreuse gold-lined 15°, 1 root beer gold luster 15°, 1 root beer gold luster 11°, and 1 root beer gold luster 15°) and pass up through the end beads, the 11°s, 4-mm rondelle, 15°s (with button on them), 4-mm rondelle, and 11°s to reinforce the clasp attachment.

3 Pass down through the end beads again, and down through 2 of the core beads in the spiral rope. Change thread direction and pick up 3 outer-color beads (1 chartreuse gold-lined 15°, 1 root beer gold luster 15°, and 1 root beer gold luster 11°), and go back up through the end beads, the 11°s, 4-mm rondelle, 15°s (with button on them), 4-mm rondelle, 11°s, and end beads. This will reinforce the clasp attachment (figure 2).

4 Pass down through 1 of the core beads in the spiral rope. Change thread direction and pick up 2 outer-color beads (a chartreuse gold-lined 15° and a root beer gold luster 15°), and pass up through the end beads, the 11°s, 4-mm rondelle, 15°s (with button on them), 4-mm rondelle, 11°s, and end beads (figure 3). After this final reinforcement, weave off the tail by half hitching several times in the outer beads of the spiral rope.

5 The loop end of the clasp is created at the other end of the necklace. To form the loop, string up 3 end beads—a 4 x 8-mm faceted glass rondelle, a 4 x 6-mm rondelle, and a 2 x 4-mm rondelle. Then pick up a series of 11°s, 2 x 4-mm rondelles, and 15°s in the following sequence: one 11°, three 15°s, one 11°, 1 rondelle, one 11°, three 15°s, one 11°, 1 rondelle, one 11°, three 15°s, one 11°, 1 rondelle, one 11°, three 15°s, one 11°, 1 rondelle, one 11°, three 15°s, one 11°, 1 rondelle, one 11°, three 15°s, and one 11°. Pass back down through the end beads and through 3 of the core beads in the spiral rope (figure 4).

6 Make sure the loop fits easily over the button at the other end of the necklace. If it seems too tight, pull the thread back through the end beads and add additional beads, continuing the same pattern until the loop fits over the button, and then pass back down through the end beads and through 3 of the core beads in the spiral rope.

7 Tapering off of the spiral is handled in a similar manner as described above for adding the button. Turn around and pick up 4 outer-color beads (1 chartreuse gold-lined 15°, 1 root beer gold luster 15°, 1 root beer gold luster 11°, and 1 root beer gold luster 15°) and pass up through the end beads and the loop beads.

8 Pass down through the end beads and down through 2 of the core beads in the spiral rope. Change thread direction and pick up 3 outer-color beads (1 chartreuse gold-lined 15°, 1 root beer gold luster 15°, and 1 root beer gold luster 11°) and go back up through the end beads, the loop beads, and the end beads. This will reinforce the loop.

9 Pass down through 1 of the core beads in the spiral rope. Change thread direction and pick up 2 outer-color beads (1 chartreuse gold-lined 15° and 1 root beer gold luster 15°) and pass up through the end beads, the loop beads, and the end beads. After this final reinforcement weave off the tail by half hitching several times in the outer beads of the spiral.

▶ Embellish the Spiral Rope

Finally on to the fun part—embellishing!! The spiral rope is embellished in 3 sections. The first, embellished with a simple bud form variation, begins at one end of the rope and covers the first 5 inches (12.7 cm) of the spiral rope. The second section, embellished with a variety of forms, fills the central 9 inches (22.9 cm) of the necklace. The final 5 inches (12.7 cm) are embellished with the same simple bud form variation as the first.

1 To begin, double thread a size 12 needle with thread approximately 10 feet (3 m) long (5 feet [1.5 m] when doubled). Weave the thread into the spiral rope, tying a couple of half hitches in the outer beads to anchor the thread. Weave your way to the first core bead. Go through this first bead, so you come out between the first and second core bead.

2 Now you're ready to begin embellishing the first section. I like to do a variation on the simple bud embellishment form. Pick up an 11°, a keshi pearl, and one 15°. Come back through the pearl and the 11° (figure 5). Pass through the next core bead, and add another keshi pearl embellishment. Add 1 embellishment between every core bead for approximately 5 inches (12.7 cm).

The center portion features an elaborate collage of floral embellishments. I combined the following embellishment forms:

- **Simple Bud** (page 27), either with freshwater pearls (figure 6) or crystal bicones (figure 7).

- **Simple Flower** (page 27), both with (figure 8) and without (figure 9) a beaded stamen made with 2 x 4-mm rondelles.

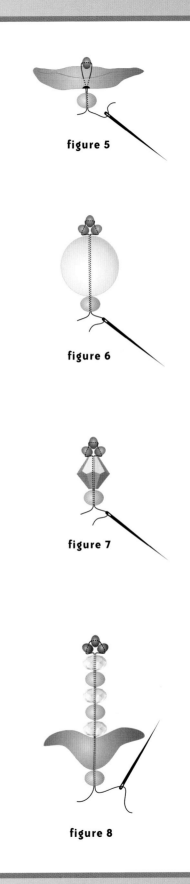

figure 5

figure 6

figure 7

figure 8

- **Berry Cluster** (page 30), made using 3-mm magatamas (figure 10)

- **Branch Fringe** (page 43), with 3-mm crystal bicones (figure 11)

- **Star Flower** (page 32), with freshwater pearls, 11°s, and 15°s (figure 12)

There's 1 embellishment between every core bead. Using a relatively large proportion of berry clusters adds considerable volume to the centerpiece. I embellish in a random order, but I do take into consideration the spacing of some of the larger embellishment forms, such as the star flowers. I space these at somewhat regular intervals throughout the heavily embellished sections. Embellishments closer to the keshi pearls are shorter, often starting with one 11° base bead on each form. The number of 11°s underneath the embellishment gradually increases as you work toward the center.

4 Begin embellishing this section with a series of simple bud and simple flower forms and then start bringing berry cluster, branch fringe, and star flowers into the mix. To unify the piece, add an occasional simple keshi pearl bud embellishment throughout the central portion of lavish embellishments. As you work toward the center of the necklace, add branching to the embellishments to thicken and lengthen the forms. Some of the forms in the middle of this section can use as many as twelve 11°s for their base stems. As you work away from the center, gradually decrease the length of the base stems and amount of branching to reduce the overall thickness and taper off the embellishing as you approach the next 5-inch (12.7 cm) section.

5 Complete the necklace by embellishing the final 5 inches (12.7 cm) with simple keshi pearl bud embellishments.

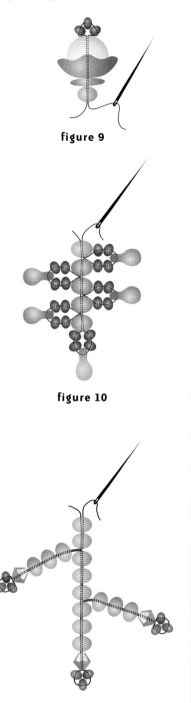

figure 9

figure 10

figure 11

figure 12

SUPPLIES

Basic Beading Kit (page 12)

Mustard-lined size 11°
Japanese cylinder beads, 2 g

Size 11° Japanese seed beads:
    Rust gilt marbled, 10 g
    Root beer gold luster, 10 g

Orange semi-matte gilt
lined, 10 g

Chartreuse gold luster size 12°
Japanese 3-cut seed beads, 10 g

Olivine silver-lined 15° Japanese seed beads, 10 g

Opaque rust luster size 15°
Japanese 3-cut seed beads, 30 g

Sterling silver size 15° Czech
charlottes, 1 g

6 opaline faceted rondelles,
2 x 4 mm

3 olivine gold luster Czech
faceted rondelles, 6 mm

Half of a 16-inch (40.6 cm)
strand of olive green side-
drilled keshi pearls, 8 x 12 mm

Burgundy red-lined 3-mm
magatamas, 20 g

INDIAN SUMMER
SUMAC NECKLACE

This necklace will teach you several versatile and useful techniques, including a few

new twists on some old favorites. The lariat neck strap is a variation of spiral rope with the

look of herringbone cording. Next, the peyote-stitched toggle clasp is a useful compo-

nent for any beaded necklace or bracelet. Finally, a variation of branch fringe creates the

berry clusters, which form the focal point of the necklace.

Note: Japanese charlottes are *much* larger than Czech charlottes; the two are not interchangeable. Be sure to use the type described in the materials list.

▶ Herringbone-Spiral Neck Strap

1 Pick up 4 rust gilt-marbled 11° core-color (hereafter referred to as CC) beads, then a series of 6 outer-color (OC) beads: 2 olivine silver-lined 15°s, 1 chartreuse gold luster 12° 3-cut, 1 root beer gold luster 11°, and 2 more olivine silver-lined 15°s. Go back up through the four CC beads to create a circle (figure 1).

2 Hold the beads in your hand so the series of OC beads is on the left and the CC beads are on the right. Pick up another series of 6 OC beads. Go back up through the 4 CC beads again, and flip this new, second set of OC beads to the right. You've completed the first full stitch (figure 2).

3 Pick up 2 rust gilt-marbled 11° CC beads, and this series of OC beads: 2 olivine silver-lined 15°s, 1 chartreuse gold luster 12° 3-cut, 1 root beer gold luster 11°, and 2 more olivine silver-lined 15°s. Slide all the beads down to the stitch base. Go through the last 4 CC beads (2 that were already there and 2 that you just added). Flip this series of OC beads over to the left (figure 3).

4 Pick up another series of 6 OC beads. Go back up through the last 4 CC beads again, and flip this new, second set of OC beads to the right. You've completed the second full stitch (figure 4).

5 Continue in this manner until the strap's the desired length.

▶ Spiral Rope Base for the Berry Cluster

Use 2 colors of size 11° Japanese seed beads— rust gilt-marbled beads for the CC, which runs down the center; the OC, which form the outer spiral, will start as root beer gold luster and then transition to orange semi-matte gilt-lined beads.

1 Single thread 1 wingspan of FireLine and wax it well. Thread 4 CC beads and 3 root beer gold luster OC beads, leaving at least 14 inches (35.6 cm) of tail at the end of the thread. Pass back through the 4 CC beads, creating a circle. Hold this base in your hand with the OC beads on the left (figure 5).

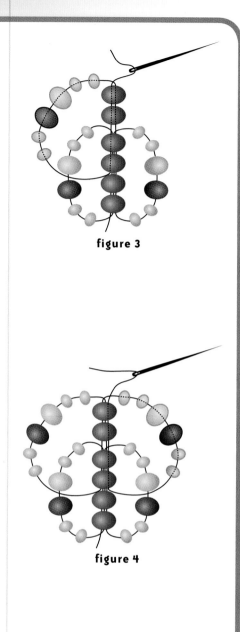

figure 3

figure 1

figure 4

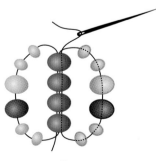

figure 2

figure 5

2 Pick up 1 CC and 3 OC beads. Slide all the beads down to the base. Circle around and pass through the 4 CC beads (3 previously added and 1 just added) (figure 6). Flip the last stitch over to the left (figure 7).

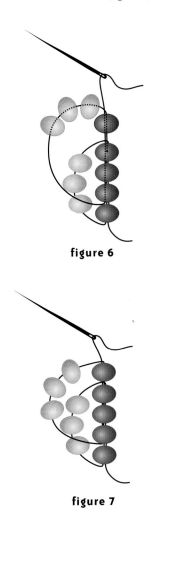

figure 6

figure 7

3 Continue to repeat this pattern, and a spiral rope cord will begin to emerge. After making about 1 inch (2.5 cm) of spiral rope using the root beer gold luster as the OC beads, switch to orange semi-matte gilt-lined beads for the OC beads. Create about 2 to 2 ½ inches (5.1 to 6.4 cm) more of spiral rope using the orange semi-matte 11°s for the OC beads. The total length of the spiral rope is 3 to 3½ inches (7.6 to 8.9 cm) long. Later, the portion of the spiral rope with root beer OC beads will be embellished with keshi pearl leaves, and the portion with semi-matte orange OC beads will be embellished with magatama-tipped berry clusters.

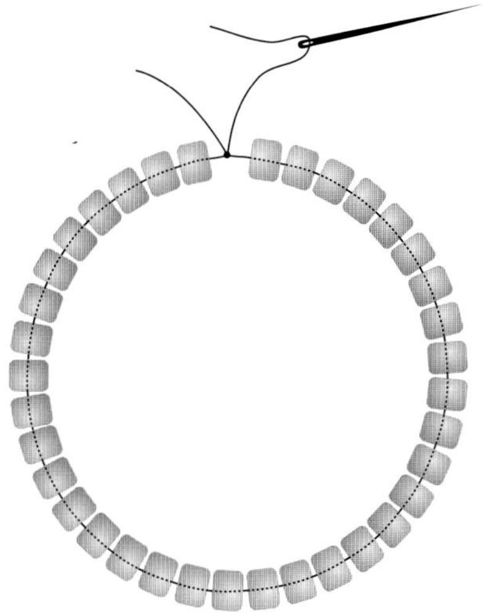

figure 8

▶ Beaded Toggle Clasp

The toggle clasp at the front of the necklace is created entirely from peyote-stitched beads and has no internal support. Begin with the toggle loop.

Toggle Loop

1 String up 48 cylinder beads on 6 feet (1.8 m) of thread. Tie a square knot to form a loop of beads, and leave a 15-inch (38.1 cm) tail (figure 8). Leave about 3 beads' width of thread showing in the loop of beads and begin peyote stitching (page 17) with cylinder beads. After doing 1 row of cylinder beads, add 1 row of 15° 3-cuts and 1 row of olivine silver-lined 15°s. Add 2 rows of 15° charlottes. As you stitch, pull each bead tightly into place to create a cupping effect.

2 Weave the working thread back to the top row of cylinder beads. Add 1 row of 15° 3-cuts, 1 row of olivine silver-lined 15°s, and 1 row of charlottes, again pulling each bead tightly into place as you stitch. Finally, zip the last row of charlottes on this side to the last row of charlottes on the first side. This pulls the sides together to form a solid loop (figure 9).

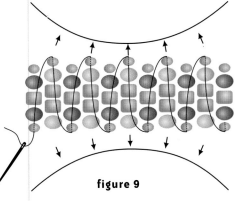

figure 9

3 Weave a toggle loop tab off the middle row of cylinder beads, 2 beads wide and 4 rows long (count 2 beads up each side).

4 To create the peyote "bead" to which the toggle loop is attached, weave a piece of flat, even-count peyote stitch 8 beads wide by 20 rows long (count 10 beads up each side). Zip the last row to the first row to create a bead. Embellish the ends of the bead with picots of 15° charlottes. Knot off and weave in the tail threads.

5 Using the thread on the toggle loop tab, zip the last row of the tab to the middle of the beaded bead. Embellish the sides of the tab with 15° charlotte picots. Knot off and weave in this thread (figure 10).

6 Weave the tail thread on the toggle loop to the center outside row of cylinder beads. Add a 12° chartreuse gold luster 3-cut between every bead in the row. This provides a finished and distinctive look to the toggle loop (figure 11).

Toggle Bar

1 String up 14 cylinder beads. Weave a section of flat, even-count peyote stitch (page 17) 14 beads wide by 12 rows long (count 6 beads up each side). Zip the first row to the last row to create a tube.

2 Embellish each end of the tube. Coming out of 1 bead at 1 end of the tube, pick up one 15° charlotte, one 2 x 4-mm rondelle, and three 15° 3-cuts. Go back through the rondelle to form a picot out of the 3-cuts. Pick up another 15° charlotte and go down through the next cylinder bead at the end of the peyote tube. Do a U-turn within the tube and come back up out of the third bead at the end of the tube. Pick up one 15° charlotte, go up through the rondelle, and through all three 3-cuts in the

picot formed previously. Go back down through the rondelle and pick up 1 more 15° charlotte. Go down through the fourth bead around the end of the tube. Repeat this process 1 more time. By using a 15° charlotte above each end bead in the tube and beneath the rondelle, it's possible to center the rondelle over the end of the tube. After completing 1 end of the tube, weave your working thread down to the other end of the tube (figure 12).

3 Repeat the process so there's a picoted rondelle at each end of the toggle tube.

4 Using either your tail thread or your working thread, weave to the center columns of the tube (seventh and eighth columns of the 14 across). Coming out of the sixth column, pick up 1 cylinder bead and go through the next bead in that row (in the eighth column). Turn around, pick up another cylinder bead, and come back through the cylinder bead previously added. Weave back and forth in this manner, creating a strip of flat, even-count peyote 2 beads wide by 20 rows long (count 10 beads up each side). Zip the last row to the base row on the tube. Embellish the edges of this loop with 15° charlotte picots. After completing the tube, weave in both threads, half hitching a couple of times before cutting the tail.

figure 10

figure 11

figure 12

▶ Attach the Clasp

In the next step, you attach everything to-gether and embellish the focal point.

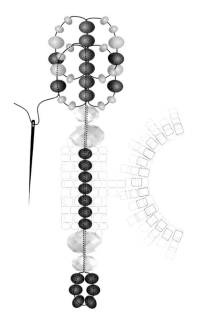

figure 13

Attach the Toggle Loop

1 Refer to figure 13 as you work. Using the tail thread on your herringbone-spiral rope neck strap, pick up one 2 x 4-mm rondelle, one 6-mm rondelle, 7 rust gilt-marbled 11°s (slide the toggle loop bead over these 11°s), one 6-mm rondelle, and one 2 x 4-mm rondelle.

2 Go down through the last 3 core beads at the root beer gold luster end of the 3-inch (7.6 cm)—or longer—section of spiral rope. Pick up 3 root beer gold luster 11°s and go back up through the 2 x 4-mm rondelle, the 6-mm rondelle, the 7 rust gilt-marbled 11°s, 6-mm rondelle, 2 x 4-mm rondelle, and up through 4 core beads in the herringbone-spiral rope.

3 Without picking up any new beads, go back down through 1 of the outer sec-tions of the herringbone-spiral rope and

down through the 2 x 4-mm rondelle, 6-mm rondelle, 7 rust gilt-marbled 11°s, 6-mm rondelle, and 2 x 4-mm rondelle. Go down through the last 2 core beads in the spiral rope. Pick up 2 root beer gold luster 11°s and go back up through the 2 x 4-mm rondelle, 6-mm rondelle, 7 rust gilt-marbled 11°s, 6-mm rondelle, 2 x 4-mm rondelle, and up through 4 core beads in the herringbone-spiral rope.

4 Without picking up any new beads, go back down through 1 of the outer sections of the herringbone-spiral and down through the 2 x 4-mm rondelle, 6-mm rondelle, 7 rust gilt-marbled 11°s, 6-mm rondelle, and 2 x 4-mm rondelle. Go down through the last core bead in the spiral rope. Pick up 1 root beer gold luster 11° and go back up through the 2 x 4-mm rondelle, 6-mm rondelle, 7 rust gilt-marbled 11°s, 6-mm rondelle, 2 x 4-mm rondelle, and up through 4 core beads in the herringbone-spiral rope.

5 Weave off this thread into the herring-bone-spiral rope, half hitching several times before cutting off the tail. Then thread up the tail thread from the root beer gold luster OC end of the spiral rope. Weave this tail into the spiral rope, half hitching several times before cutting off the tail.

figure 14

Attach the Toggle Bar

The toggle bar is attached to the other end of the herringbone-spiral rope. Refer to figure 14 as you bead.

1 Using the tail thread at this end of the herringbone-spiral rope, pick up one 2 x 4-mm rondelle, one 6-mm rondelle, and 1 more 2 x 4-mm rondelle. Pick up seventeen 15° 3-cuts. Thread the 3-cuts through the connector loop on the toggle bar and go back down through the 2 x 4-mm rondelle, the 6-mm rondelle, the 2 x 4-mm rondelle, and through the last 4 core beads in the herringbone-spiral rope.

2 Without picking up any new beads, go back up through 1 of the outer sections of the herringbone-spiral rope and through the 2 x 4-mm rondelle, 6-mm rondelle, 2 x 4-mm rondelle, and through the seven-teen 3-cuts. Go back down through the 2 x 4-mm rondelle, 6-mm rondelle, 2 x 4-mm rondelle, and through the last 4 core beads in the herringbone-spiral rope.

3 Without picking up any new beads, go back up through 1 of the outer sections of the herringbone-spiral rope and down through the 2 x 4-mm rondelle, 6-mm rondelle, and 2 x 4-mm rondelle. Pick up 17 more 15° 3-cuts. Thread them through the connector loop on the toggle bar and go back down through the 2 x 4-mm rondelle, 6-mm rondelle, 2 x 4-mm rondelle, and through the last 4 core beads in the herringbone-spiral rope.

4 Without picking up any new beads, go back up through 1 of the outer sections of the herringbone-spiral rope and down through the 2 x 4-mm rondelle, 6-mm rondelle, 2 x 4-mm rondelle, and through the second set of seventeen 3-cuts. Go back down through the 2 x 4-mm rondelle, 6-mm rondelle, and 2 x 4-mm rondelle, and then weave off the tail thread within the herringbone-spiral rope, half hitching several times before cutting the tail.

▶ Keshi Pearl Leaf Embellishments

After the necklace form is assembled, add the embellishments on the centerpiece. Using a double thread, weave into the top (OC) section of the spiral rope. Half hitch a couple of times to anchor the thread, then weave up so the thread comes out between the first and second core beads on the spiral. Add leaf embellishments between every core bead on the OC section of spiral. Two basic leaf form embellishments are used, keshi pearl leaf forms and frond forms. Mix it up by adding about 2 keshi pearl embellishments for every frond embellishment.

Keshi Pearl Leaf Forms

1 String up 6 root beer gold luster 11°s, 8 olivine silver-lined 15°s, 1 keshi pearl, and 8 more olivine silver-lined 15°s. Go back through the last two 11°s, then string up 8 more 15°s, a keshi, and eight 15°s. Go back through 2 more 11°s, then string up 8 more 15°s, a keshi, and eight 15°s. Go back down through the first two 11°s and into the next core bead in the spiral (figure 15).

Frond Forms

1 Coming out of a core bead in the spiral, string up an odd number of chartreuse gold luster 12° 3-cuts, followed by 3 silver 15° charlottes. Turn around and go back through the last 3-cut to form a picot out of the 15° charlottes. Peyote stitch back toward the base, creating a wispy, slightly curved frond-form tassel. Once you get to the bottom, go back through the next bead in the spiral rope core. Vary the length of the fronds anywhere from 7 to 23 beads; it helps create a more organic feel (figure 16).

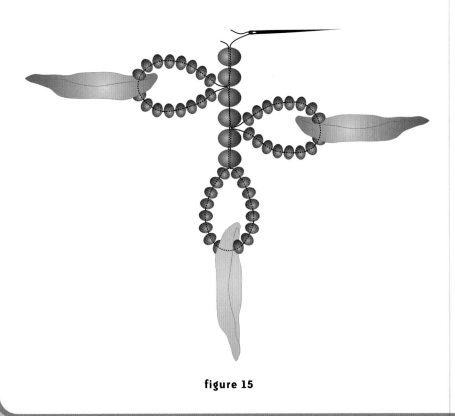

figure 15

figure 16

▶ Magatama Sumac Berry Embellishments

You'll need to add thread several times during the process of adding the leaf and berry embellishments. Weave off your old thread by half hitching several times between outer beads in the spiral. Add new thread in the same manner, anchoring it in the outer beads in the spiral. Always make knots in outer beads rather than core beads to avoid difficulties while embellishing.

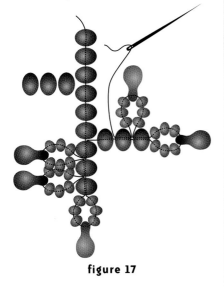

figure 17

Berry Cluster Embellishments

The berry clusters on the lariat are a variation on branch fringe (page 43), which utilizes magatamas (Japanese drop beads).

I usually begin by making several branches, each 9 beads long on the central core, branched with berry clusters. After ½ inch (1.3 cm) of these along the central core, begin branches that are 12 beads long. After doing about ¾ inch (1.9 cm) along the spiral rope of longer stems, I revert to 9-bead stems, then reduce to 6-bead stems, and then, in the last ¾ inch (1.9 cm), taper down from 5, to 4, to 3, to

2 and then 1 bead stems as I approach the end of the spiral.

1 Working downward, pick up 9 rust gilt-marbled 11°s, 3 opaque rust luster 15° 3-cuts, 1 magatama, and 3 more 15° 3-cuts. Go back through the last (the ninth) 11° of the base stem, then pick up three 15° 3-cuts, 1 magatama, and 3 more 15° 3-cuts. Go back through the eighth 11° of the base stem and pick up three 15° 3-cuts, 1 magatama, and 3 more 15° 3-cuts. Go back through the seventh 11° of the base stem.

2 Pick up 3 more 11°s to create a branch off of the base stem. Pick up three 15° 3-cuts, 1 magatama, and 3 more 15° 3-cuts; go back through the last 11° of the branch and continue to embellish with 15° 3-cuts and magatamas between each 11° on the branch. When you get back to the base stem of 11°s, return to embellishing between each bead along the base stem with the 15° 3-cuts and magatamas, until you've gone down through the fourth 11° on the base stem. Pick up 3 more 11°s to create a second branch, along which you'll embellish as described before. Once you return to the base stem, continue the embellishments down to the spiral rope base. Go through the next core bead in the spiral rope and make another embellished berry branch (figure 17).

Finish Off the End

1 Thread up the tail thread coming out of the bottom of the spiral rope. String up five 11° rust gilt-marbled beads, three 15° 3-cuts, a magatama, and 3 more 15° 3-cuts. Go back down through the five 11°s and down through the last 3 core beads in the spiral.

2 Pick up 3 semi-matte orange OC 11°s. Go up through the 11° rust gilt-marbled beads, coming out between the fourth and fifth 11°. Pick up three 15° 3-cuts, a magatama, and 3 more 15° 3-cuts. Go back down through the four 11°s and down through the last 2 core beads in the spiral.

3 Pick up 2 OC 11°s. Go up through the 11° rust gilt-marbled beads, coming out between the third and fourth 11°. Pick up three 15° 3-cuts, a magatama, and 3 more 15° 3-cuts. Go back down through the three 11°s and down through the last core bead in the spiral.

4 Pick up 1 OC 11°. Go up through the 11° rust gilt-marbled beads, coming out between the second and third 11°. Pick up three 15° 3-cuts, a magatama, and 3 more 15° 3-cuts. Go back down through the second 11° and pick up three 15° 3-cuts, a magatama, and 3 more 3-cuts. Go down through the first 11° and into the spiral. Weave off your thread, half hitching several times before cutting the tail.

POKEWEED BERRY NECKLACE

This necklace is inspired by the intriguing berry cluster forms of pokeweed. Native to New England and generally considered a weed, the plant influenced me in terms of both form and color. Although my version isn't made in the original colors of the plant, it does stay true to the berry form.

Note: Japanese charlottes are *much* larger than Czech charlottes; the two are not interchangeable. Be sure to use the type described in the materials list.

▶ Bezel the Cabochon

1 Thread up 5 feet (1.5 m) of thread on a size 13 beading needle. String up enough cylinder beads to fit exactly around the base of the cab. Count the beads in the ring; if there are an even number of beads, great. If the number is odd, add 1 more bead.

2 Tie a square knot, leaving a long tail. After knotting, loosen the circle of beads so there's 2 to 3 beads' width of thread to accommodate the tension of the first row of peyote. Working off of the initial circle of beads, peyote stitch 1 row of cylinder beads. Remember, even-count tubular peyote stitch requires a step up at the end of each row (see page 19).

SUPPLIES

Basic Beading Kit (page 12)

1 green moonstone cabochon or other stone, approximately 13 x 18 mm

Chartreuse gold-lined size 11° Japanese cylinder beads, 5 g

Size 11° Japanese seed beads:
   Metallic dark purple, 15 g
   Pale yellow opaline, 5 g

Size 15° Japanese seed beads:
   Metallic dark purple, 5 g
   Chartreuse gold lined, 8 g
   Aqua plum lined, 6 g
   Pale yellow opaline, 3 g

Gold size 15° Czech charlottes, 1 g

2 to 3 gross* of violet opal champagne crystal bicones, 3 mm

2 blue-purple freshwater pearls, 4 mm

33 or more pale yellow freshwater pearls, 6 mm

27 or more chartreuse green freshwater pearls, 4 mm

35 or more purple-black freshwater pearls, 7 to 8 mm

6 blue-purple freshwater pearls, 7 to 8 mm

12 or more magenta freshwater pearls, 4 mm

2 yellow marbled German pressed glass "mustache" flower beads, 6 x 12 mm

Amethyst green gold luster 3-mm Japanese magatamas, 5 g (used in fringing at the top of the berry clusters)

30 or more black diamond AB Czech glass drops, 4 x 6 mm (used in fringing at the top of the berry clusters)

12 or more light olivine luster Czech glass faceted rondelles, 4 x 6 mm (used in fringing at the top of the berry clusters)12 or more yellow marbled German pressed glass trumpet flower beads, 8 mm (used in fringing at the top of the berry clusters)

*Quantity depends on the desired length of the necklace.

113

3 Switch to size 15° seed beads and weave 2 rows.

4 Add 1 row of 15° charlottes to complete the back side of the bezel.

5 Weave the tail thread up to the top row of cylinder beads. Place the stone in the bezel, top side up.

6 Capture the stone by weaving 1 to 3 more rows of cylinder beads, depending on the overall height of the cabochon. When you reach the point where the stone curves in, switch to 15° seed beads. Add 2 or 3 rows of 15°s, again depending on the height of the stone. Finish off with 2 rows of 15° charlottes. As you add each row, pull each bead tightly into place to create a cupped bezel that holds the stone firmly in place (figure 1).

7 Embellish the topmost row of cylinder beads by adding 1 metallic dark purple 11° between every bead in the row (figure 2).

8 On both the right and the left side of the cabochon bezel, weave a connector tab through which the spiral rope of the neck strap will be connected to the spiral rope base of the berry cluster. The tabs should be centered directly across from each other on either side of the stone. Working out of the middle row of cylinder beads on the bezel, weave a tab of flat, even-count peyote stitch 4 beads wide by 20 rows long (count 10 beads up each side), as shown in figure 3.

9 Zip the end of the tab to the bezel base at the location where the tab originates, and embellish both sides of the tab with 15° charlotte picots.

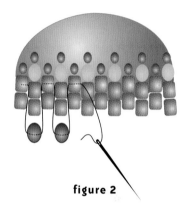

figure 1

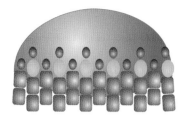

figure 2

▶ Spiral Rope Neck Strap

Make the neck strap using metallic dark purple 11°s as core-color (CC) beads, and an outer-color (OC) bead sequence composed of two 15°s (1 chartreuse gold lined and 1 aqua plum lined), 1 bicone, and 2 more 15°s (an aqua plum lined and a chartreuse gold lined).

1 Single thread a size 12 needle with 12 feet (3.6 m) of thread. Wax well. Thread up 4 CC beads and a sequence of OC beads. Pass through the 4 CCs to create a circle, leaving a 12-inch (30.5 cm) tail (figure 4).

2 Pick up 1 CC and a set of OC beads. Slide the beads down to the initial circle of beads. Count back 4 CC beads (including the just-added CC bead) and pass up through these beads. Push this last stitch over to the left. Continue adding beads in this manner until the spiral rope is half of the desired length of the neck strap. Keep in mind that the cabochon and the toggle will each add about 1 inch (2.5 cm) to the overall length, so take this into consideration when determining the length of the two halves of the spiral rope neck strap (figure 5). Leave both tail threads attached.

3 Repeat the process to create a second spiral rope for the other side of the neck strap.

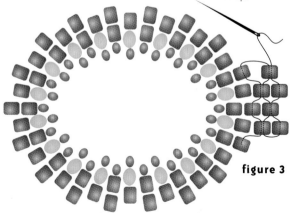

figure 3

figure 4

figure 5

figure 6

▶ Toggle Closure

This closure is the same as the one described on pages 24 and 25.

Toggle Ring

1 Following the directions on page 24, create a toggle ring starting with 36 aqua plum-lined 15°s and then adding chartreuse gold-lined cylinder beads.

2 After the ring has been zipped up, weave a connector tab 2 beads wide by 20 rows long (count 10 beads up each side). Zip the last row of the tab to the first row, and then embellish both sides of the tab with charlotte picots (page 24). Embellish the ring by adding 1 metallic dark purple 11° between every bead in the middle row of cylinder beads along the outer edge.

Toggle Bar

1 Make the toggle bar from a strip of flat, even-count peyote 14 beads wide by 12 rows long (count 6 beads up each side).

2 Zip the tab to itself to create a tube and embellish each end with a 4-mm blue-purple pearl, using the technique described on page 25. After adding the pearls, weave to the center of the tube and build a connector tab 2 beads wide by 20 rows long (count 10 beads up each side). Zip the last row of the tab to the first row, and then embellish both sides of the tab with charlotte picots.

▶ Berry Cluster Spiral Rope Base

The berry cluster spiral base is woven using a variation of spiral rope (page 20).

1 Single thread a size 12 needle with 7 feet (2.1 m) of thread. Wax well. Thread up 4 metallic dark purple CC beads and the OC bead sequence of 15° and 11° seed beads: 1 chartreuse gold-lined 15°, 1 aqua plum-lined 15°, 1 pale yellow opaline 11°, 1 aqua plum-lined 15°, and 1 chartreuse gold-lined 15°. Pass through the four CC beads to create a circle, leaving a tail about 12 inches (30.5 cm) long (figure 6).

2 Pick up 1 CC and a set of the OC beads. Slide the beads down to the initial circle of beads. Count back 4 core beads (including the just-placed CC bead) and pass up through these beads. Push this last stitch over to the left. Continue adding beads in this manner until you have approximately 3 inches (7.6 cm) of spiral rope. This will be used for the shorter, left-hand berry cluster. Leave both tail threads attached.

3 Using a new length of thread 7 feet (2.1 m) long, repeat the process outlined above to create a second spiral rope base that's approximately 4 inches (10.2 cm) long. It will be used for the longer, right-hand cluster.

▶ Add Berries and Embellishments

Begin with the shorter of the berry cluster spiral rope bases.

1 Use the shorter tail thread at the end of the spiral rope to add the end berry. Pick up 1 pale yellow pearl and 3 pale yellow opaline 15°s. Pass back through the pearl and go down through 3 core beads. Pick up the OC bead sequence less 1 bead: two 15°s, one 11°, and one 15°.

2 Go back through the pearl and the picot and pass back through the pearl again, then down through 2 core beads. Pick up the OC bead sequence less 2 beads: two 15°s and one 11°. The thread probably won't fit through the pearl again, so this time just go back down through the first core bead, skipping the pearl and picot.

3 Pick up the OC sequence less three 15°s (pick up two 15°s) and go down through the first core bead again. Tie off and weave in your tail thread.

4 Add the rest of the berries. Cut 10 feet (3 m) of thread, thread it up, and double it; wax well. Weave in this new thread, knotting on several times, and work the thread up to the tip, so it's coming out between the first and second core beads, right after where the end berry was added.

5 Begin embellishing with the pale yellow pearls: add one 11°, the pearl, three 15°s (to create a picot), and pass back through the pearl, the 11°, and the next core bead. Continue to add pearls in this manner between every core bead. For the shorter spiral, add approximately 14 pale yellow pearls. For the longer spiral, add approximately 18 pale yellow pearls.

6 Increase the number of 11°s added to the pearl embellishments as the embellishments are added up the spiral rope stem. (For a more detailed illustration of this increase, refer to page 40.) After adding the desired number of pale yellow pearls, begin adding chartreuse pearls, and finally purple-black pearls. (For the shorter spiral, add approximately 13 chartreuse pearls and 15 purple-black pearls. For the longer spiral, add approximately 14 chartreuse pearls and 20 purple-black pearls.) The pearl embellishments will cover about two-thirds of the spiral rope stem.

7 After adding a few purple-black pearls, gradually decrease the number of 11°s added to the pearl embellishments, transitioning back down to two 11°s, then one 11° underneath the pearls (as shown in the diagram on page 40), to bring in the shape of the berry cluster, until you've embellished about two-thirds of the spiral rope stem.

8 After adding the berries, embellish the top portion of the spiral rope stem with a combination of other floral embellishment forms. As shown in figures 7, 8, and 9 respectively, randomly add a combination of simple bud embellishments (page 27), berry cluster embellishments (page 30), and simple flower embellishments (page 27). Add 1 embellishment between every core bead. When adding them, vary the number of 11°s used in the stems, tapering in to create shorter embellishments as you approach the top of the spiral rope. On these last few embellishments, use magatamas and 4 x 6-mm Czech glass drops.

9 Discontinue adding embellishments about 5 core beads from the end of the spiral rope stem. Leave the working thread attached; you'll need it later to add the last couple of embellishments after the necklace has been assembled.

10 Repeat the above process with the longer spiral rope stem.

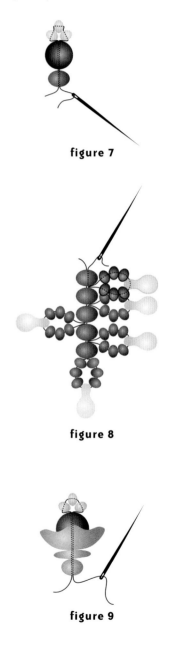

figure 7

figure 8

figure 9

116

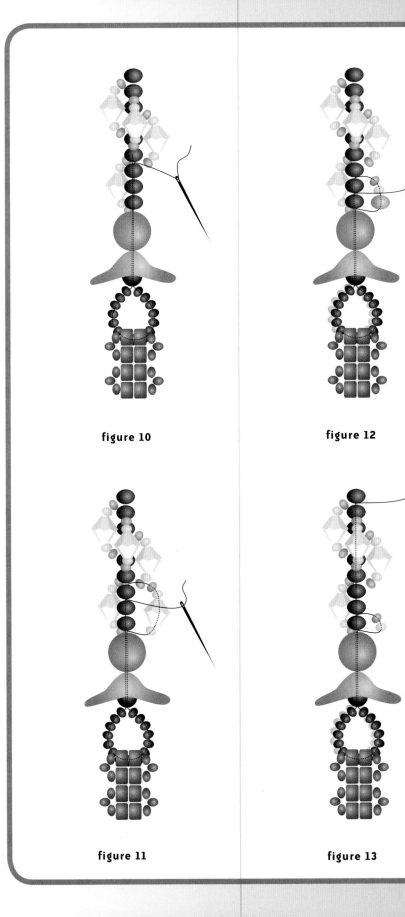

figure 10

figure 11

figure 12

figure 13

▶ Assembly

1 Begin by adding the toggle loop to the end of 1 of the bicone spiral rope neck strap halves. Thread up the 12-inch (30.5 cm) tail at the beginning of the spiral rope. String on one 6-mm blue-purple pearl, 1 mustache flower bead, one 4-mm magenta pearl, and 15 aqua plum-lined 15°s. Pass through the connector loop of the toggle loop and go back down through the magenta pearl, mustache flower, blue-purple pearl, and 3 core beads in the spiral (figure 10).

2 String up two 15°s—a chartreuse gold lined and an aqua plum lined—1 bicone, and 1 more aqua plum-lined 15°. Go back up through the end beads (the blue-purple pearl, the mustache flower, and the magenta pearl). Pass through the fifteen 15°s a second time, then go back down through the end beads and down through 2 core beads in the spiral (figure 11).

3 String up two 15°s—a chartreuse gold lined and an aqua plum lined—and 1 pale yellow opaline 11°. Go back up through the end beads. String up 15 metallic dark purple 15°s, pass through the connector loop on the toggle, and go back down through the end beads and 1 core bead in the spiral (figure 12).

4 String up two 15°s and go back up through the end beads, pass through the 15 metallic dark purple 15°s a second time, and back down though the end beads. Tie off within the spiral rope (figure 13).

5 Repeat steps 1 through 4 with the toggle bar portion of the closure, attaching it to the second section of bicone spiral rope.

6 Attach the berry cluster spirals to the neck strap spiral ropes through the loops on each side of the bezeled stone.

7 Using the tail thread from one of the bicone spiral rope neck strap halves, string up one 8-mm blue-purple pearl, pass through the loop on one side of the bezel, and thread up a second pearl. Pass down through 3 core beads in one of the berry cluster spiral ropes. String up two 15°s—a chartreuse gold lined and an aqua plum lined—1 pale yellow opaline 11°, and 1 chartreuse gold-lined 15° (figure 14).

 8 Pass up through the pearl, cab loop, pearl, and 3 core beads in the bicone spiral rope neck strap. String up two 15°s—1 chartreuse gold lined and 1 aqua plum lined—1 bicone, and 1 chartreuse gold-lined 15°. Go back down through the pearl, the cab loop, and the pearl, and down through 2 core beads in the berry cluster spiral rope. String up two 15°s—a chartreuse gold lined and an aqua plum lined—and 1 pale yellow opaline 11° (figure 15).

9 Pass up through the pearl, cab loop, pearl, and 2 core beads in the bicone spiral rope neck strap. String up two 15°s—a chartreuse gold lined and an aqua plum lined—and 1 pale yellow opaline 11°. Go back down through the pearl, the cab loop, and the pearl, then down through 1 core bead in the berry cluster spiral rope. String up two 15°s—1 chartreuse gold lined and 1 aqua plum lined (figure 16).

10 Pass up through the pearl, cab loop, pearl, and 1 core bead in the bicone spiral rope neck strap. String up two 15°s—1 chartreuse gold lined and 1 aqua plum lined. Go back down through the pearl, the cab loop, and the pearl, and weave off

the tail thread within the spiral core of the berry cluster spiral rope (figure 17).

11 Once the attachment is complete, return to the working thread on the berry cluster portion of the spiral rope and add an embellishment between each of the last few core beads to complete this side of the necklace.

12 Repeat steps 6 through 10 to attach the other side of the spiral rope neck strap to the second berry cluster spiral rope.

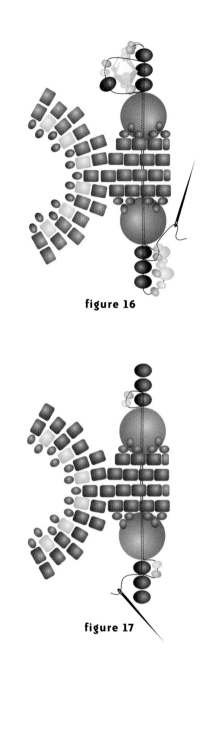

figure 16

figure 17

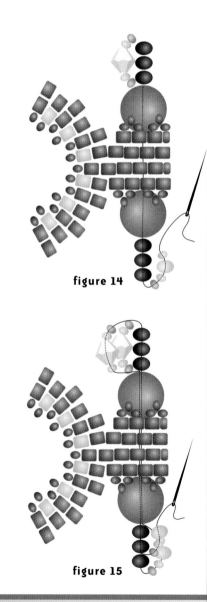

figure 14

figure 15

DAHLIA
NECKLACE

This project is a variation of the design that won me best
of show in the Bead & Button Show Bead Dreams 2003
competition. A spiral rope core is heavily embellished,
and a flower cabochon pendant made separately is
threaded onto the neck strap during its embellishment.

SUPPLIES

Basic Beading Kit (page 12)

1 black moonstone cabochon, 13 x 18 mm

Rust gold luster size 11° Japanese cylinder beads, 5 g

Size 11° Japanese seed beads:
Rust gold luster, 30 g
Topaz brick lined, 10 g

Size 15° Japanese seed beads:
Red silver lined, 5 g
Topaz brick lined, 5 g
Matte black, 15 g
Red black lined, 30 g
Rust gold luster, 5 g
Matte dark gray, 5 g

Marcasite or silver size 15° Czech charlottes, 1 g

Dark smoke topaz 3-mm Japanese magatamas, 30 g

300 dark garnet luster Czech glass drops, 4 x 6 mm

2 transparent gray black-lined Czech fire-polished beads, 6 mm

30 faceted round carnelian beads, 4 mm

30 rust orange freshwater pearls, 6 mm (used as basic bud embel-lishments on the neck strap)

40 dark gray freshwater pearls, 4 mm (used as center of star flowers and also center of basic black flower form embellishments on neck strap)

30 dark gray freshwater pearls, 5.5 mm (used as basic bud embellishments on the neck strap)

20 red center-drilled German glass flowers, 12 mm (used as larger basic flower embellishments on neck strap)

20 matte black center-drilled German glass flowers, 8 mm (used as smaller basic flower embellishments on neck strap)

Antique or new sequins (optional) (used atop the 5.5-mm dark grey pearls in a basic bud form on the neck strap)

Antique or new shank button for closure, size can vary

2 pieces of black leather, each 1 1/2 x 1 1/2 inches (3.8 x 3.8 cm)

Adhesive and toothpicks or double-sided tape

Note: Japanese charlottes are *much* larger than Czech charlottes; the two are not interchangeable. Be sure to use the type described in the materials list.

▶ Bezel the Stone

1 Glue the moonstone cabochon to a piece of leather that's about ½ inch (1.2 cm) larger than the stone on all sides. Using a toothpick, apply an even coat of adhesive to the back side of the cab. Place the glue side of the stone down on the shiny side of the leather, leaving at least a ½-inch (1.2 cm) border of leather all the way around. Allow the adhesive to dry for at least 10 minutes. **Note:** If you prefer not to use liquid adhesive, you can use double-sided tape.

2 Sew the bezel's foundation row of beads along the perimeter of the cabochon. Single thread 6 feet (1.8 m) of beading thread on a size 12 beading needle, and wax well. Tie a knot at the end and cut, leaving a ¼-inch (6 mm) tail. Pass the needle up through the leather from the back side, coming up next to the stone. Pull the thread tight so the knot is snug against the leather. String on 6 cylinder beads, slide the beads down the thread to the edge of the cabochon, place them in a line pressed snuggly against the cabochon, and then stitch back down through the leather at the end of the line formed by the 6 beads. Sew back up through the leather with the needle coming up between beads 3 and 4, and then pass through beads 4, 5, and 6 again, creating an embroidery backstitch (figure 1).

3 Continue this embroidery backstitch sequence around the perimeter of the stone. As you finish the row, make sure it contains an even number of beads; you may need to adjust the number of beads in the final stitch to accomplish this. Travel through the entire row of beads one more time without stitching into the leather, to ensure good tension.

4 Begin peyote stitching upward from the base row using cylinder beads: pick up a bead, skip a bead, go through a bead (figure 2). Continue peyote stitching with cylinder beads for a couple of rows, until you reach the curve in the cabochon. This point will vary depending on the thickness of the stone and the curvature of its dome, but you should have at least 3 rows of cylinder beads. Switch to size 15°s; the decrease in bead size will cause the bezel to curve inward, creating a tight fit around the stone. Bead 2 rows of 15°s. Pull each bead tightly into place. If the cabochon isn't securely held by the bezel, add 1 or 2 rows of 15°s.

5 Weave the thread back through the beads to the base row, and pass through the leather, knotting off on the back. With the same thread, come back up through the leather next to the outside of the foundation row of the beaded bezel. Stitch a second base row next to the bezel, using the embroidery backstitch. As you finish this row, make sure it contains an even number of beads; if necessary, adjust the number of beads in the final stitch to accomplish this. Pass through the entire row 1 more time and stitch back through the leather, knotting off on the back.

▶ Embellish the Bezel with Petals

1 Thread a size 13 needle with approximately 10 feet (3 m) of beading thread. Double the thread and knot the end, leaving a ¼-inch (6 mm) tail, and stitch up from the back of the leather into the peyote bezel. Travel up to the second row down from the top of the bezel (a row of 15°s). Add a picot of three 15° charlottes between every bead in this row (stitch in the ditch). After completing an entire round of charlotte picots, step down 1 row (figure 3).

2 In this row, add one 11° seed bead between every bead, creating bolder embellishments that offset the delicate picots in the previous embellishment round. Once this round is complete, step down 1 row (figure 4).

3 Flower petals are created by coming out between the cylinder beads in the base. String on one 11° and nine 15°s (6 topaz brick lined, and 3 red silver lined). Double back through the sixth 15° to create a picot. Begin peyote stitching (the first 2 beads are the topaz brick-lined 15°s, then 1 red silver-lined 15°). When you reach the base of the petal, turn around and pass through the first 15°, avoiding the base 11° entirely (figure 5).

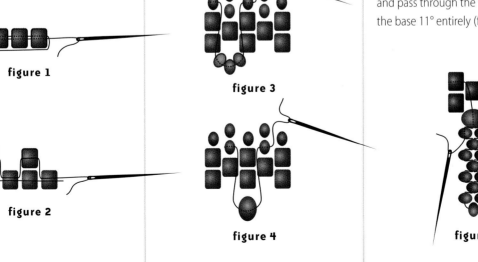

figure 1

figure 2

figure 3

figure 4

figure 5

4 Peyote stitch around the petal a second time, using only red silver-lined 15°s. Pass through all 3 beads in the picot to maintain the pointed tip (figure 6). Next, peyote stitch in 3 red silver-lined 15°s to bring you back to the base.

5 When you reach the base, turn around and step up through two 15°s to bring you to the outer edge of the petal form. Do 1 more round in red silver-lined 15°s. As you approach the tip of the petal, pass through all 5 beads at the tip (the picot and the bead on either side of it) to maintain the pointed shape (figure 7).

6 Once you finish 1 petal, go out though the base 11° and into the next cylinder bead on the bezel. Continue adding the pointed peyote flower petal embellishments in this manner until petals surround the entire bezel. Weave the working thread through the beads to the base of the bezel and pass through to the back side of the leather. Half hitch a couple of times before cutting the tail.

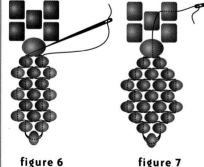

figure 6   **figure 7**

1 Single thread the needle with 6 feet (1.8 m) of nylon thread in a color that matches the leather. Tie a knot, leaving a ¼-inch (6 mm) tail. Pass the thread up through the leather between the bezel and the outer row of embroidery.

2 Using a toothpick, apply adhesive to the back of the leather, making sure not to smear any on the thread hanging from the front side. Place the second piece of leather over the back of the cabochon and press to ensure good adhesion. Allow to dry for at least 10 minutes. (If you prefer not to use glue, a small circle of double-sided tape contained within the borders of the bezel stitching will also work.)

3 Cut away any excess leather, leaving an edge the width of a row of cylinder beads.

4 Using the thread already attached to the piece, stitch both pieces of leather together using an overhand stitch, spacing the stitches about ¹⁄₁₆ to ⅛ inch (1.6 to 3 mm) apart. This ensures the backing won't separate and gives a finished look to the piece.

5 Pass the needle back up through both pieces of leather and through a couple of beads in the outer embroidered row. Working off of this outer row, peyote stitch outward, to cover up the leather edge. Do 1 row of cylinder beads and 1 row of 11° seed beads.

▶ **Bail**

1 Weave the thread through the beads and up to the top of the cabochon. Beginning slightly off of center, weave a small width (6 to 8 beads) of flat, even-count peyote stitch off of the outermost row of cylinder beads. This creates a tab that will be looped around and attached to itself to create a bail. The tab needs to be at least 28 rows (count 14 rows up each side) long to fit around the neck strap (figure 8).

2 Embellish around the stone, making varying lengths of berry cluster embellishments (page 30). Begin by coming out of the cylinder bead next to the bail; pick up three 11°s, two 15°s, 1 magatama, and 2

figure 8

122

more 15°s. Go back up through one 11°, add two 15°s, 1 magatama, and 2 more 15°s, and go through the next 11°. Repeat this process of adding the 15°s and a magatama between each 11° until you reach the top of the strand. Go through the next 11° in the peyote stitch around the stone and add another berry cluster embellishment. The length of the 11° stalks of the berry clusters will gradually become longer as you work toward the center at the bottom of the bezeled stone. Occasionally use larger Czech glass drops in place of the magatamas to add texture (figure 9).

Using a 13 x 18-mm cabochon, the sequence of the increases in the length of the berry cluster stalks added between the 11°s in the outer row is: Beginning next to the bail at the top of the bezeled stone, add 2 stalks of berry clusters with three

11°s, then 1 stalk with five 11°s, 1 stalk with seven 11°s, 1 stalk with nine 11°s, 1 stalk with twelve 11°s, 1 stalk with fifteen 11°s, 1 stalk with seventeen 11°s, 1 stalk with eighteen 11°s, 1 stalk with twenty-three 11°s, and then 1 stalk with twenty-seven 11°s. Repeat the sequence in reverse order up the opposite side of the bezel, beginning with a berry cluster stalk of twenty-seven 11°s. (**Note:** these counts will vary with different-size stones.)

3 After adding the embellishments, tie off several times within the piece, and then weave the tail down to a base row and through the leather, cutting the thread off flush on the back side. Set the cabochon aside to slide onto the neck strap later.

▶ Spiral Rope Strap

1 Single thread 60 inches (1.5 m) of thread on a size 12 English beading needle and wax well. Use rust gold luster 11° seed beads for the core-color (CC) beads and a sequence of 2 matte black 15° seed beads, 1 topaz brick-lined 11° seed bead, and 2 matte black 15°s for the outer-color (OC) beads. Begin weaving the spiral rope by threading 4 CC beads and the sequence of OC beads (figure 10).

2 Create a circle of beads by passing through the 4 CC beads. Pick up 1 CC and the 5 beads that make up the OC sequence. Circle around and pass through the 4 previous CC beads. Continue to repeat this pattern, and a spiral cord will begin to emerge. You will probably have to tie off and start a new thread several times while making the neck strap, because spiral weave consumes a lot of thread. Be sure to knot off in the outer beads, not the core beads, because you'll embellish between the core beads later and knots could obstruct your path. Bead until you have a length of spiral rope strap approximately the length you want for your finished necklace. The closure will add additional length, but embellishing will take up space on the inside of the spiral, making the necklace seem shorter.

figure 9

figure 10

▶ Button Closure

I usually add the button closure before I embellish the neck strap. Antique or new buttons make fabulous and unique closures on all types of beaded jewelry.

1 Using the tail thread that emerges from the end of the spiral, pick up one 6-mm fire-polished bead, enough 11° seed beads to equal the radius of the button, 1 carnelian bead, and 3 size 15° seed beads. Slide the button shank over the 15°s and add 1 more carnelian bead and the same number of 11°s as were used prior to threading on the button. Go back through the fire-polished bead and down through 3 core beads in the spiral rope (figure 11).

2 Pick up 4 OC beads (2 matte black 15°s, 1 topaz brick-lined 11°, and 1 matte black 15°) and go back up through the fire-polished bead, and through all the beads in the loop that attaches the button. Go back down through the fire-polished bead, and down through 2 core beads in the spiral rope (figure 12).

3 Pick up 3 OC beads (2 matte black 15°s and 1 topaz brick-lined 11°) and go back up through the fire-polished bead and through all the beads in the loop that attaches the button. Go back down through the fire-polished bead and down through 1 core bead in the spiral rope (figure 13).

4 Pick up 2 OC beads (2 matte black 15°s) and go back up through the fire-polished bead and through all the beads in the loop that attaches the button. Go back down through the fire-polished bead and down through 1 core bead. Tie off this thread within the spiral (figure 14).

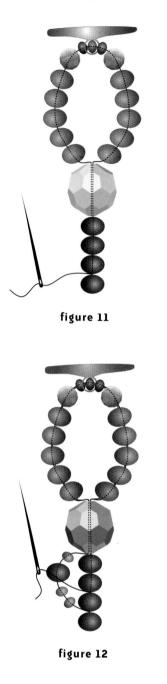

figure 11

figure 12

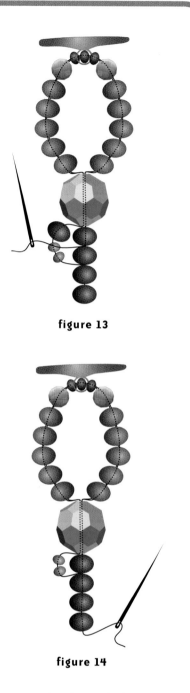

figure 13

figure 14

5 Make the button loop. Using the tail thread that emerges from the other end of the spiral, pick up a 6-mm fire polished bead, followed by an 11°, a carnelian bead, an 11°, a carnelian bead, a pearl, and an 11°. Continue picking up beads in this sequence until you've reached a length that fits comfortably over the button. Pass down through the fire-polished bead and down through 3 core beads in the spiral rope. Repeat the tapering method (steps 2 through 4) used at the other end of the spiral rope to attach the button loop. On the last pass, rather than going through the beads in the loop, pass up through the fire-polished bead and thread up a strand of 15°s (shown in grey in figure 16) to wrap around the loop. Wrap the strand around the loop beads over the carnelian beads and around the 11°s in a spiraling fashion. Make sure the strand of beads falls against the 11°s between the carnelian beads, to create a tendril form. Pass back through the fire-polished bead and tie off the thread.

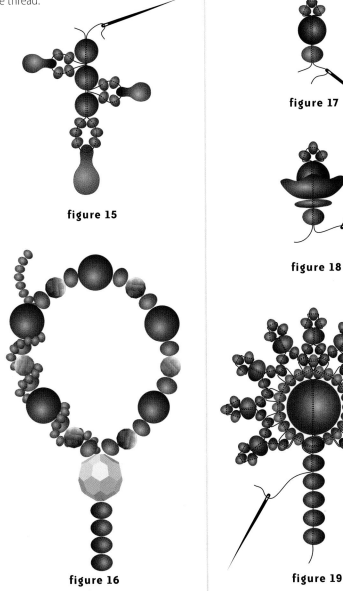

figure 15

figure 16

▶ Embellish the Neck Strap

By coming out between each spiral core bead, adding an embellishment, and stitching through the next bead, you create a lush, rich texture that's very organic.

1 Add a new double-threaded needle into the core beads of the spiral rope. Begin between the first and second bead at the end of the spiral rope and work toward the center of the spiral rope. Add 1 embellish-

figure 17

figure 18

figure 19

ment between every core bead. Some of the options for embellishment include the following, but be creative and invent your own variations and combinations.

Berry Cluster (page 30) is used to embellish around the cabochon (figure 15) using 4 x 6-mm dark garnet luster Czech glass drops as well as magatamas

Simple Bud (page 27) using 6-mm rust orange freshwater pearls, and 5.5-mm dark gray freshwater pearls (figure 17)

Simple Flower (page 27) using 12-mm red center-drilled German glass flowers, (with carnelian beads as center) and 8-mm matte black center-drilled German glass flowers with dark gray 4-mm freshwater pearls as center (figure 18)

Star Flower (page 32) using 4-mm dark grey freshwater pearls as center (figure 19).

I usually add 2 or 3 berry clusters for every other embellishment. The berry cluster embellishments decorating the spiral rope neck strap pictured here have stalks three 11°s long. I don't vary the length of the berry cluster stalks on the neck strap the way I do around the cabochon. Star flowers are the most time-consuming to make of the embellishments, so I generally do 1 every 1 to 1½ inches (2.5 to 3.8 cm) along the garland.

2 When you reach the approximate center of the neck strap, slide the embellished flower pendant onto the spiral. Weave your working thread through enough of the spiral core beads to come out right next to the other side of the bail and resume embellishing. Work your way to the end of the spiral rope

SUPPLIES

Basic Beading Kit (page 12)

1 crystal dentelle, size 60ss, or
1 crystal rivoli, 14 mm

Metallic plum size 11°
Japanese cylinder beads, 10 g

Size 11° Japanese seed beads:

Lavender opaline, 6 g

Metallic dark plum, 3 g

Size 15° Japanese seed beads:

Amethyst green gold
luster, 5 g

Matte metallic blue-
purple, 5 g

Sterling silver size 15° Czech
charlottes, 4 g

1 mother-of-pearl center-
drilled flower button, 8 mm

1 crystal bicone bead, 3 mm

Three 16-inch (40.6 cm)
strands of purple freshwater
pearls, 5.5–6 mm

Approximately 100 rose
AB crystal sequins
(a.k.a. lochrosen)

Metal shank button, size may
vary, for necklace closure

A WELL-KEPT SECRET

Create an embellished, beaded vessel pendant to hold your secret
treasures. This necklace features a complementary pearl neck strap.

Note: Japanese charlottes are *much* larger than Czech charlottes; the two are not interchangeable. Be sure to use the type described in the materials list.

▶ Bezel the Crystal Stone

Begin by bezeling the dentelle or the rivoli, which will serve as the vessel lid.

1 String up 36 metallic plum Japanese cylinder beads onto 5 feet (1.5 m) of single thread. Tie a square knot, leaving about 15 inches (38.1 cm) of tail. Once the knot is tied, loosen the circle of beads just slightly so there's about 1 bead's width of thread showing to accommodate the tension of the first row of peyote.

2 Begin peyote stitching (page 17) with cylinder beads. Add 1 row of cylinder beads, stepping up at the end of the row. You'll have 3 rows of cylinder beads (the initial circle of beads actually becomes 2 rows, and the 1 just added makes a total of 3 rows).

3 After stepping up, continue peyote stitching, this time using Japanese 15°s. Add 1 row of amethyst green gold luster 15°s and 1 row of matte metallic blue-purple 15°s. As you add each row, pull each bead tightly into place to create a cupped shape.

4 Complete this half of the bezel by adding 1 row of sterling silver 15° charlottes. This will serve as the back half of the bezel (figure 1).

5 Place the stone into the cup form, right side up. Weave the working thread up to the top row of cylinder beads.

6 Peyote stitch the top half of the bezel while holding the stone in place. Add 1 row of amethyst green gold luster 15°s, then 1 row of matte metallic blue-purple 15°s. Complete the bezel by adding 1 row of charlottes (figure 2).

7 Half hitch once or twice between the beads in the top row. This maintains the tension to hold the stone tightly in the bezel. Don't cut off any tail threads; they'll be used later.

▶ Vessel

The vessel is constructed of cylinder beads (with the exception of the upper edge), using tubular peyote stitch. Create the form by making a series of tubular peyote stitch decreases.

1 String up 11 feet (3.4 m) of single thread. Wax well.

2 Pick up 50 cylinder beads and tie a square knot to form a circle of beads, leaving about 7 feet (2.1 m) of thread as the tail. Loosen the circle of beads so there's 3 or 4 beads' width of thread showing to accommodate the tension of the first row of peyote (figure 3).

3 Pass through 2 or 3 beads to hide the knot, then begin peyote stitching with cylinder beads. Stitch a total of 7 rows (including the 2 rows formed by the initial circle of beads). Step up at the end of each row.

4 After completing the 7 rows, do the first decrease. The decrease will occur over 4 rows and reduces the circumference of the vessel by 10 beads, from 50 beads around to 40 beads around. Begin the first row of the decrease by peyote stitching the next row of cylinder beads, leaving out a bead every fifth place. To hide the thread when leaving out a bead, pass the thread down through the bead below the space and then up through the next bead. Return to regular peyote stitch for 4 more stitches before leaving out another bead (figure 4).

5 When you reach the step up, you will

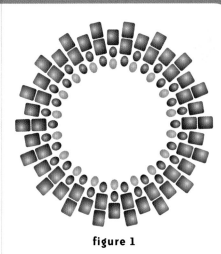

figure 1

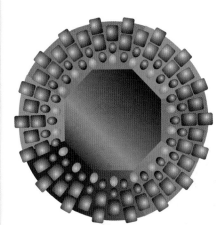

figure 2

figure 3

figure 4

pass up through 3 beads, as you're stepping up in one of the decrease voids. After stepping up for the next round (row 2 of the decrease), continue peyote stitching, but when you reach the spaces where a bead was left out in the previous row, add 2 beads to fill in the space (figure 5).

6 After the second round is complete, step up and continue peyote stitching. At the points where 2 beads were placed in the spaces in the previous row, go through these 2 beads as if they were 1 (figure 6).

7 After completing the third round, step up again to add the fourth row of the decrease. In this row, peyote stitch as normal; however, when reaching the spots with 2 "low beads," add only 1 bead over them (figure 7).

8 Add 4 more rows of regular peyote stitch (with a 40-bead circumference).

The top portion of the vessel is complete.

9 To complete the lower portion of the vessel, thread up the tail thread. Begin working downward by executing another 4-row decrease, as described above in steps 4 through 7, to reduce the circumference from 50 beads to 40 beads. The decreases should be placed in line with the decreases on the upper portion of the vessel (figure 8).

10 After completing the 4-row decrease, add 1 more row of regular peyote stitch, then begin another decrease, this time decreasing the circumference from 40 beads to 30 beads. Accomplish the decrease in the manner described above, but this time leave out every fourth bead. Again, the decreases should be placed in line with the previous decreases.

11 Add 1 more row of regular peyote stitch. Then complete another 4-row decrease, which reduces the circumference to

20 beads. Follow the decrease directions described in steps 4 through 7, but leave out every third bead.

12 Add 1 round of regular peyote, then do another round of decreasing, to reduce the circumference to 10 beads this time leaving out every other bead.

13 Step up and put 1 bead (rather than 2) to fill in the gap. This helps pull in the bottom of the vessel. After completing this row, step up and then pass through the 5 "up" beads of the previous row, without putting any beads in between. Pass through these 5 beads several times to tighten everything up.

▶ Attach the Lid

1 Before making any attachments, embellish the top of the bezel with lavender opaline 11° seed beads. Add one 11° between every bead in the topmost row of cylinder beads in the bezel (figure 9).

2 Weave a strip of flat, even-count peyote stitch 4 beads wide by 3 rows long (count 1 bead up one side and 2 beads up the other) off the center row of cylinder beads on the bezel. This tab will serve as the hinge.

3 To weave the tab into the vessel's top row of cylinder beads, center it along 1 of the 5 sides of the pentagonal vessel and zip it into place (figure 10). Using the attached thread, add one lavender opaline 11° between every cylinder bead in the top row of the vessel, except where the tab is attached (see figure 9). Follow this with a second row of charlotte picots along the top of the vessel. These two rows create a "lip" for the lid to fit into.

Embellish each side of the tab with charlotte picots. Leave a tail thread attached to the lid.

figure 5

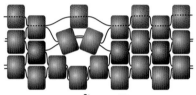

figure 6

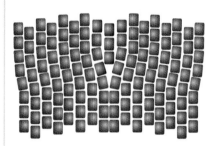

figure 7

figure 8

figure 9

128

Handle

1 The vessel hangs from the neck strap by a handle. To form it, begin weaving by coming out of the second row of cylinder beads from the top, a quarter of the way around the vessel's circumference from the hinge. Weave a strip of peyote stitch 2 beads wide by 96 rows long (count 48 beads up each side). Attach the end of this strip to the same row of cylinder beads on the opposite side of the vessel directly across from the beginning of the strip. Embellish each side of the handle with charlotte picots (figure 11).

Bail

Attached to the handle is a bail that ensures the vessel hangs with the front side forward.

1 Using cylinder beads, weave a strip of flat, even-count peyote stitch 6 beads wide by 60 rows long (count 30 beads up each side).

2 Thread the strip through the handle, then zip the last row of the strip to the first row of the strip and embellish the edges with 15° charlottes.

Add the Button

The flower button is attached to the vessel directly opposite the lid hinge, in the first row of the decrease on the top side of the vessel.

1 Coming out of the first row of the decrease on the top of the vessel, pick up 2 11°s, the mother-of-pearl button, a 3-mm crystal bicone, and three 15° seed beads. Go back down through the bicone, the button, and both 11°s and into the next bead on the same row in the vessel. Reinforce the button attachment by passing the thread through the beads of the button attachment a couple more times (figure 12).

2 Return to the tail thread left attached to the vessel lid. Weave the thread through the bezel until it comes out of a bead in the middle row of the bezel, directly across from the hinge. Thread up enough 15°s to form a loop that fits comfortably around the button. Go back into the next bead in the same row of the bezel. Reinforce the button loop by passing the thread through the loop a couple more times.

Embellish the Vessel

To create the appearance of a grape cluster, add a tail of pearl clusters coming out of the bottom of the vessel. Add these embellishments using FireLine, because the edges of the holes of the crystal sequins added on top of each pearl are sharp and could cut through other threads.

1 Coming out of 1 of the 5 "up" beads in the center bottom of the vessel with a double thread on a size 13 beading needle, add 10 or so (depending on how long you want the cluster to be) lavender opaline 11° seed beads. These form the stalk to which you'll add the pearl embellishments. Pick up 1 metallic dark plum 11°, 1 pearl, 1 crystal sequin, and three 15° charlottes. Go back through the sequin and the pearl—creating a picot of the charlottes—and up through the next 11° in the stalk (figure 13).

2 Tighten the thread and then add 1 metallic dark plum 11°, 1 pearl, 1 sequin, and three 15° charlottes. Go back through the sequin, pearl, and 11° and up through the next 11° in the stalk. Continue in this manner until you reach the base of the vessel.

3 Weave back into the vessel. Around the bottom edge of the vessel randomly add

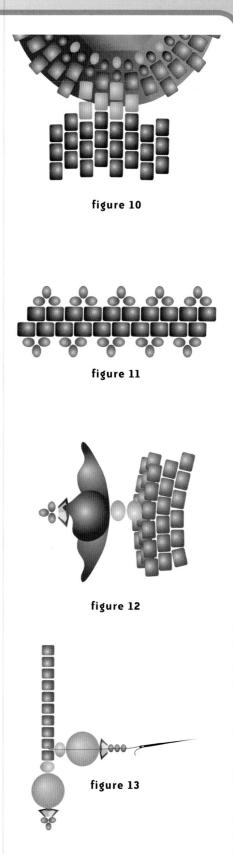

figure 10

figure 11

figure 12

figure 13

5 sets of 3 grapes (which are made by simple branching using 11°s, freshwater pearls, crystal sequins, and 15° Czech charlottes) (figure 14). There's no set pattern for where to add these. Space them approximately equidistant from each other along the bottom edge of the vessel.

4 Cover the entire surface of the vessel with randomly spaced single grape embellishments composed of one 11°, 1 pearl, 1 sequin, and a picot of three 15° charlottes (figure 15).

▶ Necklace

1 Single thread 7 yards (6.4 m) of thread onto a size 13 English beading needle. (I recommend using either B-weight nylon thread or 4-lb. FireLine for this part.) String up one 11° and center it on the thread. Pass through it again to make it a stop bead. Thread on 1 pearl, one 15° charlotte, 1 amethyst green gold luster 15°, 1 matte metallic dark blue 15°, 1 lavender opaline 11°, 1 matte metallic dark blue 15°, 1 amethyst green gold luster 15°, and one 15° charlotte. Continue threading up this sequence (adding a pearl and seed beads) until all of the pearls from one 16-inch (40.6 cm) strand of pearls have been strung. Complete stringing the strand with a pearl (figure 16).

2 Thread on twelve 15°s after the pearl, then pass through the shank of the button and go back through the pearl (figure 17).

3 String up the following seed bead sequence: one 15° charlotte, 1 amethyst green gold luster 15°, 1 matte metallic dark blue 15°, one lavender opaline11°, 1 matte metallic dark blue 15°, 1 amethyst green gold luster 15°, and one 15° charlotte, and pass through the next pearl. Continue in this manner until you reach the stop bead.

There should now be 2 sets of seed beads between every pearl.

4 Remove the stop bead and thread up enough seed beads (alternating one 15°, one 11°, etc.) to fit comfortably around the button at the other end of the strand (figure 18).

Pass back through the end pearl and again add sets of seed beads between the pearls all of the way to the button end of the strand. Leave this tail attached and thread a size 13 English beading needle onto the tail thread at the button loop end of the strand (figure 19).

5 Go through the end pearl and pass through the beads in the button loop, and back through the end pearl. Heading toward the button end of the necklace, do another pass, adding the seed bead sequence between each pearl. When this step is completed, there should be 4 sets of seed beads between each of the pearls.

6 Go through the loop of beads holding the button and back down through the pearl. Make one final pass, adding the seed bead sequence between each pearl. The finished neck strap will have 5 sets of seed beads between each of the pearls.

7 Tie off the tail threads within the button and the button loop, half hitching twice before cutting the tail. Thread the necklace through the vessel pendant's bail twice, creating a double-strand neck strap.

figure 14

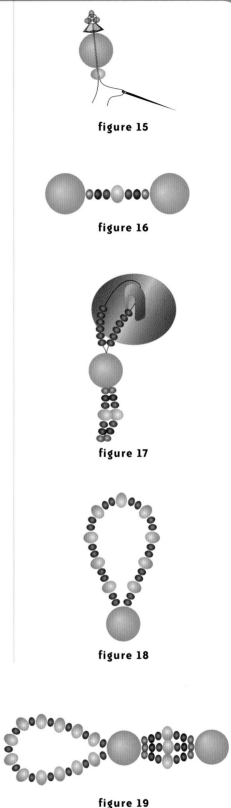

figure 15

figure 16

figure 17

figure 18

figure 19

SUPPLIES

Basic Beading Kit (page 12)

Matte metallic 24-karat gold size 11° Japanese cylinder beads, 2 g

Matte metallic silver size 11° Japanese seed beads, 5 g

Size 15° Japanese seed beads:

   Matte metallic 24-karat gold, 2 g

   Opaline 24-karat gold lined, 2 g

   Matte metallic silver, 10 g

   Clear 24-karat gold lined, 2 g

   Opaque black, 5 g

Metallic 24-karat gold size 15° Czech charlottes, 4 g

3 black freshwater pearls, 8 mm

Metallic blue green 3-mm magatamas, 10 g

APRIL SHOWERS NECKLACE

Here's a great everyday piece so elegant it works for more formal occasions, too. With its cascading floral focal point, it teaches how to work Ndebele stitch off of peyote stitch, and how to create three-dimensional forms off of an Ndebele base.

Note: Japanese charlottes are *much* larger than Czech charlottes; the two are not interchangeable. Be sure to use the type described in the materials list.

▶ Center Ring

First, create the center ring component, using tubular, even-count peyote stitch (page 19).

1 String 48 cylinder beads onto 6 feet (1.8 m) of thread using a size 13 English beading needle. Leaving a 20-inch (50.8 cm) tail, tie a square knot to form a loop of beads. Leave a gap about 3 beads wide with the thread showing in the loop and begin peyote stitching with cylinder beads.

2 Stitch 1 row of cylinder beads.

3 Stitch 2 rows of 15°s, the first with matte metallic gold and the second with opaline 24-karat gold lined.

4 Stitch 2 rows of 15° charlottes, pulling tightly as you stitch to create a cupping effect.

5 The first side of the ring is complete. Weave the working thread back to the top row of cylinder beads. Beginning here, add 2 rows of 15°s and 1 row of charlottes, again pulling in with each consecutive row.

6 Zip the row of charlottes on this side to the second row of charlottes on the first side by zigzagging through the high beads of each row; the 2 sides will come together to form a solid loop.

7 After completing the ring, add the center axis with the pearl. Coming out of the center row of charlottes along the inside of the ring, pick up two 11°s, 1 pearl, and 2 more 11°s. Go through the charlotte directly opposite the one you came out of originally, do a U-turn, pass back through the 11°s, the

pearl, and the 11°s, and back through the original charlotte out of which you began the axis (figure 1). Use a size 15 needle if necessary.

▶ Begin the Ndebele Tubes

The ring and the cascade are connected to each other using 2-ladder tubular Ndebele, worked directly off of the beaded ring. The Ndebele neck straps are also attached to the ring in the same manner. The secret to working Ndebele off of a peyote base in a seamless manner is to begin the Ndebele tube base between 2 beads along the center row of cylinder beads in the ring.

1 Weave your working thread to the middle row of cylinder beads on the beaded ring— at the space that is at a 90° angle from the pearl axis. Pick up 2 matte metallic silver 15° seed beads and go through the next bead.

2 Coming out of this cylinder bead, weave diagonally up to the next cylinder bead, do a U-turn, and come back in the other direction through the cylinder bead directly below the one you just went through. Pass back through the second cylinder bead between which the 15°s were added.

3 Pick up 2 more matte metallic silver 15° seed beads and go back into the original cylinder bead out of which you came in step 1. These four 15° seed beads will serve as the basis for a 2-ladder tube of Ndebele, which will become the base of the pagoda cascade (figure 2).

4 Add the base beads for 2 more Ndebele tubes for the neck straps. This is done in the following manner: add 6 picots of 15° Czech charlottes (a picot is simply a "small point" formed by picking up 3 beads before passing through the next bead in the working row). This puts you in the correct position to add the Ndebele base as you did in steps

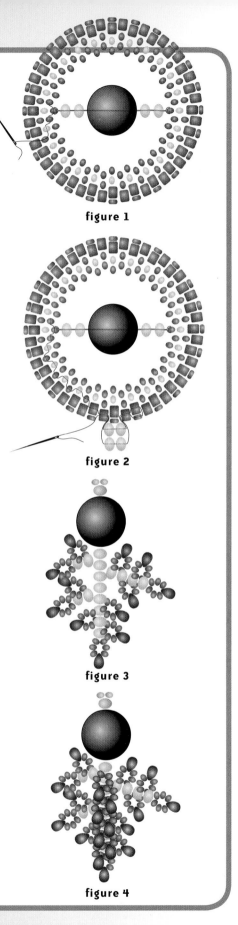

figure 1

figure 2

figure 3

figure 4

1, 2, and 3. After adding the Ndebele base, add 9 picots along the outside of the ring. Add another Ndebele base following steps 1, 2, and 3. Add 6 more picots along the outside of the ring, which will bring you back to the Ndebele base for the cascade. The neck strap tubes should be 7 center row cylinder beads away from the cascade base, which will put them slightly above center in relation to the ring axis.

▶ Cascading Floral Drop

1 Using your working thread, start the pagoda cascade by working off of the start of the Ndebele tube on the bottom of the ring. Weave 40 rows of Ndebele (page 21) using the matte metallic silver 15°s. You're ready to add the pearl and the branch fringe at the bottom of the cascade.

2 Coming out of the first bead in the first ladder of the fortieth row of Ndebele, pick up 1 matte metallic silver 11°, 1 pearl, 8 matte metallic silver 11° seed beads, three 15° charlottes, 1 magatama, and 3 more 15° charlottes. Pass back up through 1 of the eight 11°s added after the pearl. Add 3 charlottes, 1 magatama, and 3 charlottes; go back up through the next 11°, then re-peat twice more. Coming out of the stem, add a branch (page 43) two 11°s long. Add a magatama (with charlottes on either side) at the end of the 2 beads and turn around to go through the 11°. Add a magatama, go through the next 11°, and then back into the stem. Pass up through a couple of beads, then create another branch four 11°s long. Add 1 magatama (with charlottes on either side) at the end of the branch. Continue adding magatamas between the 11°s of the branch. When you get back to the stem, pass through 2 stem beads and add the final branch, which is 2 beads long (figure 3).

3 Go back up through the pearl and 11° into the second bead in the first ladder of Ndebele. Go through the first bead in the second ladder of Ndebele and travel down through the 11°, the pearl, the 8 base 11°s, the charlottes, the end magatama drop, and the charlottes. Go back through the eighth 11° and work your way back toward the pearl, adding 1 magatama drop between each 11° on this central base strand. Go through the pearl and the 11° and through the second bead in the second ladder of Ndebele (figure 4).

▶ Bell Flower

Make the bell flower at the base of the cascade using the technique described on page 47.

1 To get in position to make the bell flower at the bottom of the cascade, travel with the working thread up through ten 15°s in the ladder of Ndebele.

2 Do 1 round of Ndebele in opaline 24-karat gold-lined 15°s, adding 2 beads on the 2 ladders of Ndebele, and adding 2 beads between each ladder, resulting in 4 ladders that protrude from the original Ndebele tube in matte silver (figure 5).

3 Again using opaline 15°s, step up and begin another round, this time adding 2 beads to each of the 4 ladders, and also adding 1 bead between each ladder (figure 6).

4 Step up and do another round of Ndebele in the same color, adding 2 beads to each of the 4 ladders and adding 2 beads between each of the 4 ladders (figure 7).

5 Step up and begin another round of Nde-bele in opaline, adding 2 beads to each of the original 4 ladders and adding 2 beads to

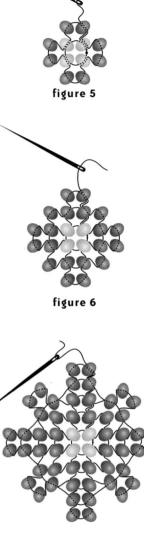

figure 5

figure 6

figure 7

the 2 "between ladder beads" to create another Ndebele ladder between each of the original 4, for a total of 8 ladders (figure 8).

6 Step up and complete 1 more round of 8-ladder Ndebele with the opaline 24-karat gold-lined 15°s before switching color.

7 Do 3 rounds of clear 24-karat-gold-lined 15°s, then switch to the matte metallic 24-karat gold 15°s and do 2 rounds of these. Do 1 round of black 15°s.

8 Create the flared bottom by stepping up from the row of black 15°s and adding a final row, with only one 15° charlotte atop each ladder of Ndebele and a magatama between each ladder.

▶ Pagoda Forms

1 To begin the bottommost pagoda, travel up through 2 rows of the Ndebele tube from the top row of the bell flower. Do a round of Ndebele with black 15°s, adding 2 beads atop each ladder and 2 beads between each ladder.

2 Working off of these 4 ladders, do another round of Ndebele with black 15°s, picking up 1 bead between each ladder.

3 After this row, continue doing Ndebele on each ladder, but use peyote stitch (page 17) between each ladder. With each row, the peyote stitch will increase by 1 bead between each ladder, creating the flared appearance (figure 8). As you add rows, the form will begin to develop 2 distinct downward-oriented points and 2 upward-oriented points.

4 Do 2 rows of matte 24-karat gold 15°s, 1 row of clear 24-karat gold-lined 15°s, 1 row of opaline 24-karat gold-lined 15°s, and a final row of black 15°s, with the following changes to the pattern: Add two 15°s, a magatama drop, and 2 more 15°s on

top of the Ndebele towers that point down, and add a single 15° on top of the Ndebele towers that point up.

Weave back to the top row of the pagoda and travel up through 8 matte silver 15°s in the original Ndebele tube to get in position to make the second pagoda from the bottom. It will be 1 row smaller than the first one.

5 Do 2 rows of black 15°s, 1 row of matte 24-karat gold 15°s, 1 row of clear 24-karat gold-lined 15°s, 1 row of opaline 24-karat gold-lined 15°s, and a final row of black 15°s, with the following changes to the pattern: Add two 15°s, a magatama drop, and 2 more 15°s on top of the Ndebele towers that point down, and add a single 15° on top of the Ndebele towers that point up.

Weave back to the top row of the pagoda and travel up through 8 matte silver 15°s in the original Ndebele tube to get in position to make the third pagoda, which will be 1 row smaller than the second pagoda.

6 Do 1 row of black 15°s, 1 row of matte 24-karat gold 15°s, 1 row of clear 24-karat gold-lined 15°s, 1 row of opaline 24-karat gold-lined 15°s, and a final row of black 15°s, with the following changes to the pattern: Add two 15°s, a magatama drop, and 2 more 15°s on top of the Ndebele towers that point down, and add a single 15° on top of the Ndebele towers that point up.

Weave back to the top row of the pagoda and travel up through 8 matte silver 15°s in the original Ndebele tube to get in position to make the top pagoda. This will be 1 row smaller than the third pagoda.

7 Do 1 row of matte 24-karat gold 15°s, 1 row of clear 24-karat gold-lined 15°s, 1 row of opaline 24-karat gold-lined 15°s, and a final row of black 15°s, with the fol-

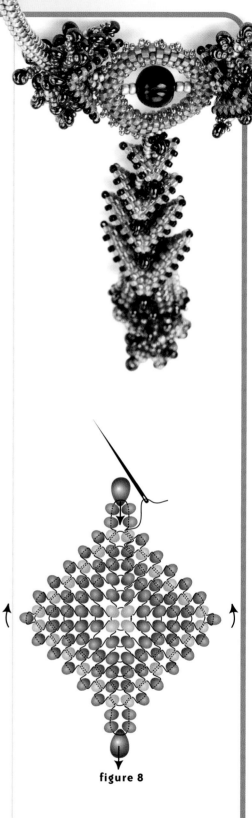

figure 8

lowing changes to the pattern: Add two 15°s, a magatama drop, and 2 more 15°s on top of the Ndebele towers that point down, and add a single 15° on top of the Ndebele towers that point up.

Weave back to the top row of the pagoda and travel up through 5 matte silver 15°s in the original Ndebele tube.

8 You're ready to make the final embellishment of the floral cascade. On the front and back sets of beads at the base of the Ndebele tube, add 2 black 15°s, 1 magatama, and 2 more black 15°s.

▶ Neck Strap

1 Once the cascade is complete, return to the sets of 4 beads added to the ring earlier and intended for the neck strap. Using these beads as the base of a 2-ladder Ndebele tube, weave a tube that's the desired length for your sizing on either side of the ring.

▶ Embellish the Neck Strap

The pagodas on each side of the beaded ring are made using the same technique as was used for the second-from-the-bottom pagoda in the cascade.

1 Add a new thread by the center ring and weave up through 3 matte silver 15°s in the Ndebele tube to arrive at the starting position for adding this pagoda. Follow the row count and bead sizes and colors from the instructions in step 5 of Pagoda Forms above.

2 The embellishment that sits inside these neck strap pagodas is accomplished using simple branch fringe (page 43) with magatamas, as was done at the bottom of the cascade. Weave through 2 matte silver 15°s from the top inside of the pagoda and

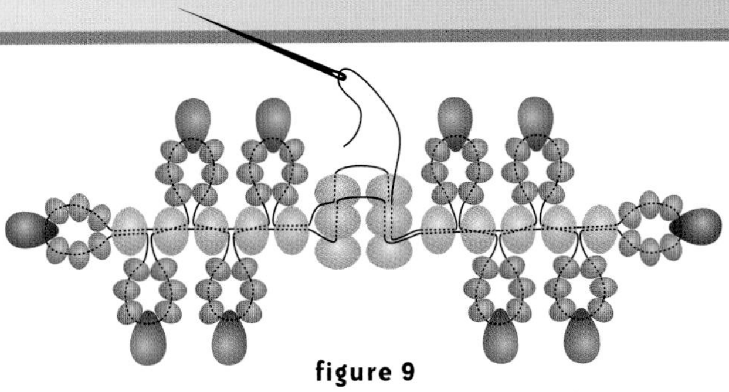

add 2 branch fringe forms using five 11°s for the central stems and magatamas for embellishments. The branch fringe forms are directly across from each other on the Ndebele tube (figure 10).

3 Weave up through 2 more matte silver 15°s in the Ndebele tube base and add 4 branch fringe forms, each three 11°s long and embellished with magatamas, on all 4 sides of the neck strap (figure 11).

4 Weave up through 2 more matte silver 15°s and do a final round of 4 branch fringe forms, this time just adding the charlottes and drops between each of the 4 beads in the tube (figure 12).

▶ Button Closure

The button—a pearl—and button closure loop are added to the ends of the neck straps, which are then finished with a pagoda form. It's easier to add the button closure first, and then add a pagoda that is the same size as the second-from-the-bottom pagoda in the pendant (step 5).

1 To add the button, come out of the first bead in the first ladder of the top row of Ndebele, add 5 matte silver 11°s, a pearl, and 3 matte silver 15°s. Go back down through the pearl and the 11°s and into the second bead in the first ladder of Ndebele. Go up through the first bead in the second ladder of Ndebele, through the 11°s, the

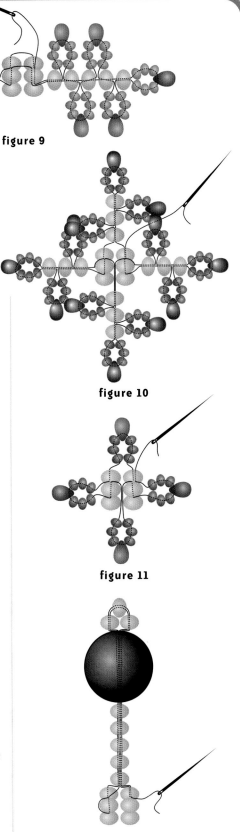

figure 9

figure 10

figure 11

figure 12

pearl, the 15°s, back through the pearl, and through the 11°s. Go into the second bead in the second tower of Ndebele (figure 13). Add the pagoda, beginning at the end of the Ndebele strap.

2 To add the loop end of the closure, come out of the first bead in the first ladder of the top row of Ndebele and add a series of beads in the following order, repeating until the loop fits snuggly around the pearl: one 11°, 3 matte gold 15°s, 1 matte silver 11°, 3 matte gold 15°s, one 11°, etc. When the loop is the proper length, go into the first 11° and the second bead in the first ladder of Ndebele. Go up through the first bead in the second ladder of Ndebele and back through the 11° and the closure loop and into the second bead in the second tower of Ndebele (figure 14). Add the pagoda, beginning at the end of the Ndebele strap, following the same steps as was done on the button end.

3 Knot off several times with half hitches and hide the threads before cutting off any remaining tails.

Laura McCabe

Georgian Jewels, 2009

15.2 x 17.8 x 2.5 cm

Vintage Swarovski crystal stones, glass seed beads, freshwater pearls; peyote stitch, herringbone, embellishment

PHOTO BY MELINDA HOLDEN

figure 13

GALLERY

This section showcasing pieces by other artists demonstrates the versatility possible with embellished beadwork.

TOP

Cynthia Rutledge

Tibetan Bangles, 2003

7 x 7 x 2.5 cm

Delica beads, seed beads, semiprecious stone beads, Czech glass rondelles; brick stitch, peyote stitch, embellishing techniques

PHOTO BY MARK RUTLEDGE

CENTER

Gregory Hanson

Victorian Cuff, 2008

19.5 x 9 cm

Cylinder beads, seed beads, vintage nail heads, Czech charlottes, crystals; peyote stitch

PHOTO BY ARTIST

BOTTOM LEFT

Carol Wilcox Wells

Ruffled Lace, 2008

Length, 73.7 cm

Japanese glass seed beads, Swarovski crystals, stones, beads, assorted sew-ons; tubular herringbone stitch, peyote stitch, chevron chain stitch

PHOTO BY SCOTT POTTER

David K. Chatt

Bubble Bowl, 1996

17.8 x 22.9 x 17.8 cm

Glass seed beads, thread armature; improvised right-angle weave

PHOTO BY JOE MANFREDINI

BOTTOM

Carol Perrenoud

Bead My Valentine/Spikes, 2000

4 x 4 x 2 cm

Seed beads, bugle beads, stuffing; brick stitch, picot stitch, edging

PHOTO BY ARTIST

TOP LEFT

Lisa Klakulak

Snap, 2008

11.4 x 7.6 x 1.3 cm

Silk fabric, wool fleece, reclaimed
snaps, shell beads, glass seed
beads, waxed linen, cotton thread;
bead stippling, wet felted, hand
stitched

PHOTO BY TOM MILLS

TOP RIGHT

Joyce J. Scott

Day After Rape II: Bosnia, 2008

21.6 x 20.3 x 5.1 cm

Seed beads, thread; peyote stitch

PHOTO BY MICHAEL KORYTA

BOTTOM

Teresa Sullivan

Wanted on Six Planets, 2008

33 x 18 x 2.5 cm

Seed beads; sculptural peyote
stitch, netting

PHOTOS BY DAN KVITKA

140

TOP

Heidi Kummli

Sacred Path, 2004

35.6 x 20.3 x 2.5 cm

Seed beads, wood; bead embroidery

PHOTOS BY ARTIST

RIGHT

Sherry Serafini

Rusted Heart, 2009

45 x 21 x 2 cm

Crystals, Japanese seed beads, pearls, metal; bead embroidery

PHOTOS BY LARRY SANDERS PHOTOGRAPHY

BOTTOM

Jonna Faulkner (art clay)
Marcie Stone (beadwork)

Tidepool Bracelet, 2005

16.5 x 7 x 5 cm

Art clay silver focal point and button, seed beads, pearls, garnets; sculptural peyote stitch

PHOTO BY GREGORY HANSON

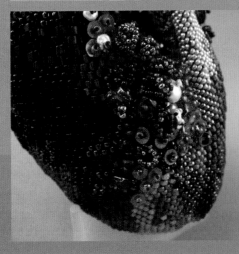

TOP RIGHT

Fran Stone

Purple Haze, 2006

22.9 x 15.2 cm

Antique and modern seed beads, pearls; Ndebele stitch

PHOTO BY GREG HANSON

BOTTOM LEFT

Marcie Stone

Reef Pod, 2009

12.5 x 7 x 6 cm

Thermoplastic resin, vintage and modern seed beads, pearls, garnets, crystals; peyote stitch

PHOTOS BY GREGORY HANSON

ABOUT THE AUTHOR

PHOTO BY MICHAEL MCCABE

Laura Jean McCabe is a primarily self-taught beadweaver with an education in anthropology and historical costume reproduction and restoration. Her elaborately beaded body adornment combines Native American, African Zulu, and Victorian beadweaving techniques with modern materials and color schemes. She shows in both national and international beadwork exhibitions, and sells her finished work at boutiques and galleries throughout the United States and on her website, www.lauramccabejewelry.com. Laura maintains a working studio in Mystic, Connecticut, and teaches beading workshops in the United States as well as around the globe.

142

ACKNOWLEDGMENTS

Without the support, encouragement, and patience of so many people, this book would never exist. I'd like to take a moment to thank just a few of them . . .

First and foremost, I must thank my husband Michael, to whom this book is dedicated. Without his endless support, I wouldn't be where I am today. His patience, love, and understanding, along with his artistic appreciation, have made my life with beads possible.

I'd also like to extend my infinite gratitude to Gregory Hanson, my technical editor and—more important—close friend, who has been so fundamentally involved in the development of this book. I'm also forever grateful for the friendship and advice of his wife, Marcie Stone,

the individual responsible for my teaching career. She's the first person I ever taught for, and the one who convinced me to continue on after that first time.

Many thanks to my amazing studio assistants, Brandi Glaza and Lilli Brown. Their dedication to "the cause" is immeasurable, not to mention the day-to-day encouragement and friendship they provide. Without them, I wouldn't be able to teach, travel, and design to the extent I'm now able.

A heartfelt thanks goes out to my editor at Lark Books, Nathalie Mornu. Without her patience, encouragement, and great organizational skills, this book would never have come together.

Thank you to my family and friends, and to Po for her constant presence throughout the writing process.

Last, but by no means least, thank you to all my students, who have helped me refine my writing and teaching skills. Without their inspiration, enthusiasm, and support, this book wouldn't have come to fruition.

INDEX

143

Laura McCabe

Sharkfin Bracelet, 2009

17.8 x 5.1 x 7.6 cm

Glass seed beads, crystal beads, custom-cut Savannah jasper by Gary
Wilson lapidary), 14-karat gold slide clasp; peyote stitch, embellishment
PHOTO BY MELINDA HOLDEN

OTHER BOOKS IN THIS SERIES

Diane Fitzgerald's Shaped Beadwork

Along with color, texture, and luminosity, shape can set a piece of jewelry apart. In this book, the renowned beading teacher shows you how to weave simple increase patterns to make beautiful two- and three-dimensional forms. Some of the projects consist of creating a single bead in a specific shape—a lovely triangle bead is given extra dimension with the addition of bezeled cabochons, for example, or six square pieces are joined to create a cube bead and then embellished with nailheads and faux bezels. Most of the projects offer instructions for making complete pieces of jewelry. The versatile patterns the author provides are building blocks that you can use to design your own inspiring jewelry.

Diane Fitzgerald is the 2008 recipient of the Bead & Button Show Excellence in Bead Artistry Award. She has taught bead classes across the United States and internationally since 1989. She's the author of numerous books devoted to beads and beadwork.

Marcia DeCoster's Beaded Opulence

Right angle weave is an essential, versatile stitch for creating fantastic beadwork. In this book, the popular beading teacher presents more than 20 magnificent contemporary jewelry projects to make with right angle weave. From the elegant Etruscan Treasure necklace to the sophisticated Fanfare bracelet, Marcia's skill-building projects will teach you how to create supple beaded fabric, beaded ropes, shaped curves, and embellished layers. Complete with an inspiring gallery of right angle weave work by other important artists, this beautifully photographed book will enable you to make spectacular pieces of eye-catching complexity and depth.

Marcia DeCoster's work has been featured in many leading magazines and publications. She teaches workshops in the United States and internationally.